ENDURING SUCCESS

HOW TO STAY AT THE TOP IN BUSINESS

SIR STEVE REDGRAVE

headline
business plus

First published in Great Britain in 2010 by
HEADLINE PUBLISHING GROUP

1

Cataloguing in Publication Data is available
from the British Library

ISBN 978 0 7553 1966 4

Typeset in Stone Serif by Avon DataSet Ltd,
Bidford on Avon, Warwickshire

Printed and bound in Great Britain by
Clays Ltd, St Ives plc

HEADLINE PUBLISHING GROUP
An Hachette UK Company
338 Euston Road
London NW1 3BH

www.headline.co.uk
www.hachette.co.uk

CONTENTS

INTRODUCTION

The language of sport and the language of business have a lot of vocabulary in common. Whether it's teamwork, goal setting, rivalry, management, talent, preparation or hard graft, the similarities are obvious and numerous. Since I retired from rowing in 2000, I have been asked to visit companies throughout Britain and across the world to share insights from my career and show how sporting tactics can also help achieve success in business.

I have had the privilege of working with some of the biggest and most well-known businesses in the world, as well as some smaller ones that most people won't have heard of. While I hope they have learnt something from listening to me speak, I have received quite an education from meeting their teams and seeing how they operate. Within ten minutes of arriving at a company's HQ or annual awards event I can usually tell if the staff are motivated, fulfilled and dedicated. When you visit as many companies as I do, you develop an instinct about which organisation is on its way up, which is stagnating and which is struggling.

In recent years, I've noticed that the questions I am asked at my public speaking engagements are less likely to be about achieving success; they are more often about holding on to it. In the past decade, Britain seems to have gone through a business revolution. TV shows like *The Apprentice* and *Dragons' Den* are watched by millions of people, and the decade that began with the dot-com bubble and ended with the credit crunch has meant business and finance have rarely been out of the news. As a consequence, we've become very business literate and many of the people I address from the corporate sector have already heard speeches from other people along the lines of 'how I made it' or read books about how they can boost their careers. What they increasingly want me to tell them is how they can use insights from my twenty-five-year career in sport to help them maintain their position at the top. When people in business have attained a certain level of income, status or power, they are very keen not to see that level drop.

Over the past couple of years, I've looked more closely at the people I've met in business as well as in sport and tried to work out how they have achieved enduring success. I've analysed my own track record, and looked to find the qualities and attributes that mark individuals and companies out for long-term success.

I've been incredibly fortunate to interview some remarkable people for this book whose insights into business I have the deepest respect for. They are all exceptionally successful people, and most of them are also very wealthy. When you meet people who have enough money in the bank to do whatever they want for the rest of their lives, there is an obvious question you have to ask them: why do you carry on? Most of us, I think, would be tempted to take the next flight to the Caribbean and find a stool at the bar if we were in their position.

Of course, success isn't about wealth. My dad ran his own business for thirty years. It never made him a millionaire, but it paid enough for him to raise three kids, employ several people and pay off his mortgage. Do I think he's a successful businessman? You bet. His ambition was to earn enough to take care of his family. Success, to me, is achieving what you set out to achieve. The financial rewards are secondary.

My interest in business has been life-long. As well as my dad's business – a construction firm and, for a time, a garden centre – my mum was also self-employed and worked as a driving instructor. While there was never a family business that, as their only son, I was expected to take over like a plot from *Dynasty* or *Dallas*, the idea that – whoever you work for – you ultimately work for yourself was ingrained into me and my sisters from a young age. As a teenager I had my own landscaping business that fitted in with my training, and if I had ever been forced to give up sport due to injury, I would probably have gone back to it.

Since my retirement from rowing, I've been involved in launching a couple of businesses. My FiveG clothing brand, which was set up in 2001, now sells fair trade cotton menswear in branches of Debenhams and is now expanding into womenswear. I've also been heavily involved in launching Juice Doctor, a range of isotonic fruit drinks. I've learnt an awful lot from my business partners in these ventures, but I'd like to think that they have also been able to learn from the experience I've gained from competing at the top level of my sport.

In business, as in sport, you have to take responsibility for your actions. You get out what you put in and if you don't get the results you wanted, it's probably because you haven't worked hard enough. I sometimes wonder what I would have done if I hadn't started rowing, and subsequently started winning. I look at the career of Peter Jones, from *Dragons' Den*, who is just a couple of years younger than me and grew up a few miles away. Like me he is tall and athletic, and he too had a teacher who encouraged him to take up a sport. In his case it was tennis. Perhaps he knew he would never be good enough to compete in major tournaments and instead he set up a tennis academy. This early taste of business gave him the appetite to become incredibly successful, not to mention wealthy.

Sport and business define success very differently. In sport, fourth is nowhere. I've even heard of people throwing away silver medals. For a lot of athletes, winning is the only thing that makes sense of competing. Business is different. In business you can be the thirtieth most successful entrepreneur in the country, or your industry, and still be considered a phenomenon. I think it is precisely because the benchmarks in sport are so high, and so transparent, that the skills and knowledge we acquire from competition are so highly valued by the businesses that pay to hear people like me speak.

In sport you can't hide behind your figures, or bury your shortcomings in the small print. While you might be able to get away with a few cheats in business in the short term, in the long term a badly run business will always fail. That's why the people I've profiled for this book have run their businesses for over twenty years: I wanted to see if the qualities that have kept them at the top are the same as those needed to excel in sport.

The things that drive you to succeed when you have everything to gain are very often very different from the things that motivate you when you have nothing left to prove. What we gain from studying the people who have stayed at the top of their game for twenty years or more, is a perspective that helps us all to be more successful. In my sporting career, so much of my life was focused on one event, often years in the future, that I frequently forgot what I would do the day after the race I had trained for. I have seen almost as many people in sport fall apart after a victory as I have after a loss. By focusing on short-term goals, we risk losing control and direction. The long-term view offered in these pages also helps to put setbacks into perspective.

I have heard many people say over the years that to succeed, you must first plan to succeed. I agree with them, and I would add that if you intend to succeed in the long term, you must first plan to succeed in the long term.

1

THE VISION THING

In sport, it's usually pretty obvious what your goal is: to achieve a personal best, to beat your rival, to win a gold medal. In business, goals are often more arbitrary – to improve sales figures by 10 per cent, to win a new contract, to increase efficiency. They can be a little uninspiring because, let's face it, if you don't win a contract this week, there will usually be a chance to win another one next week. In sport, especially in Olympic sports, the opportunities for progress and victory are so few that every race, every bout, every match matters. Sport is harsh like that – in business, you tend not to be punished quite so severely when you have an off day. So how do you get motivated to reach your goals when they seem to be of relatively little significance?

The secret is to make your goals meaningful. The way most companies do it is by making their corporate goals mean something to the workers whose job it is to make them a reality. A 10 per cent lift in sales figures becomes a bonus or a pay rise, a client's signature on a new deal becomes a night out on the boss's credit card: whether it's a new car or an 'employee of the month' certificate, businesses have found ways of incentivising their workforce to achieve their goals. The most successful organisations are adept at dovetailing their workers' goals with their wider corporate goals.

> When companies and individuals fall short of their targets, it is often because they weren't sufficiently inspired by their goals.

We all work harder, and better, when the goal we are working towards means something to us. If winning a contract means not losing your job, or training harder means making the Olympic qualifying time, or losing weight means fitting into your wedding dress, goals with consequences push us towards success. When companies and individuals fall short of their targets, it is often because they weren't sufficiently inspired by their goals. Identifying and connecting with your goals is the foundation of success. If you are not achieving the level of success you had hoped for, an analysis of the goals you have set yourself is the first place to look to make changes. Ask yourself how you can make them more meaningful.

There are several ways you can do this. When goals are unattainable they lose their power to inspire us, and breaking them down into achievable targets gives them the potency they previously lacked. Alternatively, adding a specific reward or punishment to a goal can also get you motivated, which is why saving up for a deposit on your first flat is more likely to see money accumulate in your account than if you decide simply to 'save money'. Conversely, in training, I would some-times tell myself that if I didn't make a certain time in training, I would have to repeat the session, or punish myself with an extra hour in the gym.

Sometimes, though, it's simply that we have set ourselves goals that are never going to inspire us to achieve: if you don't care about getting a promotion, or don't mind one way or another if your company meets its end-of-year growth targets, these goals are never going to help you find success. If you, your company or your team are underachieving, look carefully at the goals you have – or, perhaps more crucially, have not – set. Take the time to analyse the things you want – at work, at home, in your social life – that actually mean enough to you to motivate you.

However, goals alone don't help businesses achieve *enduring* success, because if all employees care about is a slightly larger pay packet or a better venue for the Christmas party, what's to stop them moving to companies that also offer those things? High staff turnover rarely works out for either the employee or the employer: the former never stays anywhere long enough to make enough of an impression to succeed, and the latter gets caught in a cycle of hiring that is costly and inefficient.

In my experience of visiting companies and talking to their leaders and employees, there is a clear difference between those businesses that have goals, and those that have vision. Goals bring short-term gains, but – as in sport – it is vision that sustains you over the long haul. Put another way, goals are what you do, and vision is who you are. Goals get you to the top, vision keeps you there.

Vision statements

I was recently asked to give a motivational talk to employees at the UK headquarters of Panasonic. I confess to not having known a great deal about the company beyond the obvious fact that it makes stereos and TVs, but once inside their offices, I couldn't help but notice posters of the founder, a man called Konosuke Matsushita. These posters included what, in corporate speak, would be called a 'vision statement'. I found it really quite interesting.

> Recognising our responsibilities as industrialists, we will devote ourselves to the progress and development of society and the well-being of people through our business activities, thereby enhancing the quality of life throughout the world.

Pretty grand stuff! I had expected to read something about making the best electronics equipment, or the cheapest, or a desire to become the biggest electronics firm. I was so intrigued that I asked the guy showing me round to tell me something about the founder. He launched into a story about how, in 1918, Matsushita had invented a double socket for light bulbs and started selling them from his house. Five years later he invented a second product – a bicycle lamp. By 1935, Panasonic produced over 600 different products. These days, he told me, the company makes more than 15,000 products and, not-so-incidentally, has a turnover of over $50bn.

My trip to Panasonic really stayed with me, and in the days afterwards I couldn't get the story of Matsushita out of my head. Surely, I found myself asking, when he was inventing his double light bulb socket, he hadn't had the vision to 'enhance the quality of life throughout the world'. I tried to join the dots between his first product and the current business and started to see just how important vision has been to companies like Panasonic, and began to analyse how it underpins enduring success.

The founders of the world's largest and oldest corporations couldn't possibly have known that their businesses would endure and thrive for so long. In many cases businesses start off in one field and transition into another: for example, Nokia, the mobile phone company, started out as a manufacturer of paper and rubber products. I don't suppose that its founder

Fredrik Idestam had a vision of the mobile future when he sold his first pair of Wellington boots any more than I knew that I would win gold medals at five consecutive Olympics when I first took an oar in my hands. Even Bill Gates, when he famously predicted that one day there would be 'a computer on every desk and in every home', surely can't have foreseen just how integral computers would have become to all our lives just a couple of decades on. So what is this vision thing, then? If it's not short-term goals and it's not a dreamlike premonition of the future, what exactly is it?

I certainly didn't have it when I first started rowing at the age of fourteen. An English teacher at my school was a rowing fan and he selected a handful of pupils each year to get in a boat and give it a go. Even though I had grown up in Marlow, a town on the banks of the River Thames, and had seen crews going up and down the water throughout my childhood, I'd never thought to join them. When I started rowing, I initially saw it as a chance to muck about with my mates rather than sit in a classroom. At first I never even thought about racing, but our teacher, Francis Smith, started entering us for races, and in our first year we won every single race! Maybe this is when I first had an inkling that rowing might be more than a hobby, but I certainly didn't picture myself standing on a rostrum with a medal round my neck as the national anthem played.

As I moved up through the junior ranks, I started to realise that I was probably the best rower for my age in the country, and it was then, when I was in my late teens, that I first got a glimpse of my future as an Olympic champion. However, it wasn't as a rower – it was as a sculler. Originally my plan was to compete in the single sculls, but when my results as a single sculler fell short of Olympic standards, I was encouraged to move back into rowing. I came close to taking part in the 1980 Olympics in Moscow, but a partial boycott by Britain meant only a handful of athletes got on the plane. It became my goal to compete at the Olympic Games of 1984, soak up the atmosphere, learn from the experience and have a better shot at winning gold four years later. At twenty, that was my ambition: get experience under my belt and aim for gold in the 1988 Olympics. My dream – my goal – was to win one Olympic gold medal.

However, when I went to the 1984 Olympics in Los Angeles, our coxed four – myself, Martin Cross, Richard Budgett, Andy Holmes and Adrian Ellison – unexpectedly won. Suddenly my dream had become winning *another* Olympic gold. Even when I was training to compete in my fifth Olympics, in Sydney in 2000, my dream wasn't to win a fifth gold medal, it was to win the gold medal that I didn't already have. The question I'm most frequently asked is where I found the motivation to go for gold a fifth time – and the answer is vision.

In the year after an Olympics, when the next race that matters is nearly four years away, it is harder to motivate yourself to get out and train. Whether it's runners pounding the streets, cyclists clocking up the miles, swimmers in the pool at 5 a.m. or rowers getting their boat out on to the icy winter water, it is something other than a distant goal that makes them do it. Those athletes that continue to train just as hard in the year after an Olympics as they do in the months before have a vision of themselves that sustains them. They see themselves as a particular type of competitor, someone who finds their identity in the journey, not just the destination.

My vision was of an athlete who was the best in his sport, and my dedication to being the best was integral to that vision. *It* was who *I* was. Like a professional, I trained two or three times a day; I even ran from my house to the river and back so I could fit more training in. This was going beyond what the sport required at that time but it was how I saw myself as a competitor.

Goals change

The problem with relying on goals to lead you to success is that they change. What inspired you when you were fifteen is unlikely to inspire you when you are thirty-five, so unless your goals evolve with you, they will lose their ability to motivate you. Even if you don't change, the world around you changes, and I frequently encounter businesses that are pursuing goals and targets that have become meaningless. What's the point in having a target to increase CD sales when the world has moved on to MP3s? When your goals lose their power, it's your vision that sustains you.

In my experience, you can tell which businesses and professionals have a vision of themselves to back up their short-term targets. In my charity work, I have met individuals who see themselves as campaigners: they don't simply want to raise money, they want to fight injustice and will not stop until their battle is won. You can just see it in their eyes – the fight is who they are. And when I visit companies or make a speech at their annual award ceremonies, you can really tell which business is there to make money, and which is there because it believes in what it is doing and has truly found a purpose.

Which brings me back to Panasonic. It was really

telling that the guy showing me round knew his company's history. I don't know how long he had worked there, but it certainly wasn't long enough for him to have been boxing up the double light bulb sockets! Nevertheless, he knew his company's story. Those posters on the wall communicated something to employees and they felt a part of something.

There's not much point having a vision unless it's communicated. One of the things I see a lot in businesses is CEOs and managers who cannot understand why their staff aren't getting the results: their problem isn't that their staff are lazy or stupid, simply that there is poor communication between the board room and the shop floor. In the best companies, people are working for something more than their pay cheques: if the entire team can share a vision, then they can make faster, better progress. This is where the analogy with sport is so useful. What's the point of a team manager devising a strategy or a set piece if his players don't know how to follow through?

Obviously in a rowing team of four, or a football team of eleven, communicating vision is much easier than when you have 15,000 employees, but successful businesses find ways of instilling a piece of the founder's vision, or the chief executive's goal, into every member of staff. Take McDonald's. Sometimes in my career when

I've been taking part in regattas in countries where the food and hospitality at the event has been, how can I put this politely, *unappetising*, I have found myself standing outside a branch of McDonald's knowing that if I step inside, I will get a meal I can rely on. I know that the Big Mac in Bucharest will taste like the Big Macs I've had in London. I remember once sitting in a McDonald's in a country I'd never been to before and tucking in to a burger that made me feel like I was home, and wondering how McDonald's managed to maintain consistency over both decades and distance. The answer lies in their channels of communication. Every new employee is part of the 'crew' (they are actually called crew members) and their training systems are so well developed that McDonald's can keep rolling out identikit restaurants.

Vision is essential, but only a shared vision ensures continuing success.

Case study
Name: Rupert Murdoch
Business: News Corporation
Years in business: 58

On 4th February 1989, there were four TV channels in

the UK. On 5th February, there were eight. It doesn't sound like many now, but the doubling of the number of TV channels overnight created quite a stir at the time and the man behind that stir was Rupert Murdoch.

Murdoch is a divisive figure, and he was particularly so in the late 1980s. A few years earlier he had broken the print unions when he moved the headquarters of his newspaper empire out of Fleet Street to new offices in Wapping. Mentioning Murdoch's name at a party was a quick way of finding out someone's political stance. For some, particularly some in the media, the fact that Murdoch was behind Britain's new satellite TV service was a reason to deride it.

And the critics found plenty to deride. There was the programming, of course, which was low-budget and imported. Although Sky launched with a movie channel, the fact that its signal was unencrypted meant the big studios wouldn't let it show their films. The big sporting events were already on ITV and the BBC, so the secondary events on Eurosport were hardly a big draw. However, the thing that really made the critics doubt Murdoch's wisdom was that only a few hundred households in Britain had a satellite dish. Commentators were sure Murdoch had just made the most expensive mistake of his career.

I've never met Rupert Murdoch, but from everything

I've ever read about him, I don't suppose he cared what anyone else thought. Why? He had vision. When the rest of the nation was still getting to grips with Channel 4, Murdoch saw a multichannel future. In America, shopping channels, music channels and news channels were well established and some of them – MTV, CNN – were making millions for their owners. Murdoch's plan was to expand his media empire from print into television. After all, he reasoned, why shouldn't the UK have the same number of channels as the US?

In fact, there had always been a very good reason why not: regulation. Commercial television was regulated by the Independent Broadcasting Authority, but by broadcasting via communications satellites, Murdoch circumvented the IBA's area of control which meant the only barrier to launching more channels was money. And that was something Murdoch had plenty of. He was so sure of his vision of the future of television that he was prepared to use his profits from the *Sun*, the *News Of The World* and the *Times* newspapers to bankroll his new TV empire. It was estimated at the time that Sky was costing him £2m a week.

It's easy to see why: the cost of setting up Sky was enormous. He built studios in west London for his new twenty-four-hour news station, he started his own direct sales operation to sell dishes when the high street names didn't push them hard enough, he pioneered the call-centre-based customer service operations that are so familiar now and he invested in encryption technology that meant he could do deals for big films from big studios. And he did all this at a time when hardly anyone could receive his channels.

Dish sales crept up to around 10,000 new subscribers a month, but Sky would need millions of subscribers to make money. Even with 10,000 new customers a month, Sky would go bust before it had a chance to turn a profit. In fact it very nearly did: in the recession of the early 1990s, advertising revenue slumped at Murdoch's newspapers, and it was only because he sold magazine titles he owned in America that he was able to keep Sky afloat. One of the other things Murdoch did in the early years of Sky was to 'merge' with the only other satellite operator in the UK, British Satellite Broadcasting. Both companies were losing money and they could not afford to compete against each other and so a deal was agreed. Although officially it was called a merger, it effectively amounted to a takeover of BSB by Sky.

Then in 1992, Rupert Murdoch saw a really big opportunity to make those who still derided him to sit up and take notice: when the TV rights for the new FA Premier League came up for sale, Murdoch stunned everyone by offering £304m for a five-year deal. It was way more than ITV had paid previously to screen live football matches, and by taking the nation's favourite sport off free-to-air television, millions of football fans were now persuaded to take out a subscription to Sky. Murdoch had found a way to share his vision of a multichannel future: now pretty much everyone in the country realised satellite TV, and Sky, was here to stay.

Murdoch's career started in the early 1950s when after studying at Oxford University he returned to his native Australia to take over the running of the *Adelaide News*, a newspaper owned by his late father. From there he went on to buy other papers in Australia, and later started acquiring them in the UK (including the *Sun*, which he bought in 1969 when it was making a loss and on the verge of being closed down) and the US. He now owns movie studios, newspapers and satellite networks across Asia, and Sky has 8 million subscribers paying an average of £366 a year.

Murdoch's vision wasn't just about satellite TV and the future of the media; it was the vision he had of himself that proved so important. Like a lot of Australians, he has little regard for convention. Just as when the Aussies play the Poms at cricket, Murdoch saw himself as the outsider battling against the Establishment. When critics labelled Sky TV as 'council house TV' he argued in a speech that 'much of what passes for quality on British television is no more than a reflection of the narrow elite which controls it and has always thought that its tastes were synonymous with quality'. Similarly, when his tabloid newspapers were labelled the gutter press, he defended his publications by saying: 'I'm rather sick of snobs who tell us they're bad papers, snobs who only read papers that no one else wants.'

He saw himself as someone who would shake up convention, whether that was breaking the unions or building a satellite empire from scratch. He was a corporate bruiser who could take any bullying that was dished out because that was how he saw himself. 'I'm a catalyst for change,' he once claimed. 'You can't be an outsider and be successful over 30 years without leaving a certain amount of scar tissue around the place.'

His vision of himself as an outsider, as a maverick, allowed him to push through changes most CEOs would be neither brave nor stubborn enough to do. The more vitriol that media commentators poured on him, the more determined he became. He knew that when you upset the apple cart, you tend to get hit with some rotten fruit. His vision of himself meant that every time he got knocked, he took it as further evidence that the Establishment needed shaking a little bit harder. Whether you like him or loathe him, it's hard not to admire him.

2

FINDING YOUR TALENT

In business there's a saying that you'll find profits where the skills fit the opportunity. It's true in sports too: where you can fit the athlete to the sport, you stand a far greater chance of success. There's a reason why sprinters and long-distance runners have different physiques: some of us are good at some things, some of us at others. The key to success is finding out where your particular talents lie.

I consider myself very lucky to have found rowing. If I had gone to a different school where my English teacher didn't have a love of the sport, the chances are I would never have got in a boat. I don't doubt that I would have played other sports – I was extremely competitive, even as a teenager – but if I had made the football or rugby teams, would I have made it to international level? Would my physique have been the same advantage in those sports as it was in rowing? Once I'd got in a boat, I soon discovered that I was capable of producing an explosive force at the beginning of races; would I have discovered a similar asset in another sport? Would I have enjoyed being in a team of eleven rather than a smaller team of two or four? I'm a bit of a loner, so I even think I was suited to the solitary aspect of ploughing up and down the river, too exhausted to make conversation. My natural talents and my personality were a great fit with rowing. Years of hard training then improved my talent. When you can align your talents with your occupation, you can stick it out for the long haul.

Of course, talent is only one component of success, and the history of sport – as well as business – is filled with the names of champions who took the bare bones of talent and fleshed it out with technique, effort and determination. I don't think you can achieve success without talent, but that doesn't mean you have to be the most talented person in your field to reach the top. Take the decathlete Daley Thompson: even though he retired from competitive sport twenty years ago, he's probably still in the running to be called Britain's greatest athlete (and I'm pretty sure he'd think he deserves such a title!). He won back-to-back gold medals at the Moscow and Los Angeles Olympics in 1980 and 1984 and at times he simultaneously held every international title *and* the world record. He was an icon of British sport throughout the 1980s but I think – and he might even admit this himself – he would have preferred to have been a 100m sprint champion, but the fact was he wasn't fast enough.

However, he also had a talent for throwing a shot put and a javelin and, if he really pushed himself, he could haul his sturdy frame round the track for the 1500m. Daley Thompson's talent was being good at ten different disciplines rather than excelling in one. He then trained fantastically hard to become the best all-rounder of his era.

As with Daley, it's not always obvious to spot, or discover what your true talent is. I have a friend who used to work in the media, and one of his colleagues was forever coming up with 'brilliant' ideas for new TV shows. My friend thought he was talentless in comparison, but after a couple of years of working with the idea generator at the next desk, he finally realised where his true talent lay: his skill was picking the one idea in a hundred that was worth pursuing. His judgement was his defining talent: in an industry where everyone thinks their ideas are wonderful, his ability to pick the right projects has been invaluable, and he has gone on to have a very successful career as an agent where his primary role is spotting other people's talents.

> Spending time analysing your strengths and natural abilities, you find yourself a place where you can shine.

Your talent may not be immediately apparent, or if it is, it might not be obvious how it can help your career or your business, but spending time analysing your strengths and natural abilities, and by seeing how – like Daley Thompson – you can combine raw talent with dedication and training, you find yourself a place where you can shine.

While it's possible to find short-term success in a role to which you are not naturally suited, I think there's a limit to how long people can swim against the tide. The people who sell their businesses rather than grow them may well be people who know their talent for their field will only get them so far. Enduring success requires, I believe, a pretty tight fit between talent and circumstance.

That's because when you find that fit, you also find

something else: passion. We all like to be good at things. You don't, for instance, find many people who are passionate about fly fishing if they haven't at least had some success with the rod. It's not often you find someone with a passion for something that they have no talent for. And when you find people with an exceptional talent, you frequently find an exceptional passion.

The psychology of it is pretty obvious. Just as a dog learns to fetch and roll over with praise and the promise of biscuits, when we receive praise for doing something, we tend to do a lot more of it. The more praise you get for being good at something, the more you want to do, and the more your passion for it grows. The combination of talent and passion is powerful because they feed one another.

My passion for rowing was enough for me to force myself to spend endless hours on the river and in the gym, and the harder I trained, the better I got or, you could say, the more talented I became. In endurance sports, sheer dedication can get you to a very high level, and the harder you train the better you will do. More time in the gym means bigger muscles which means more power. More passion means more talent, which means more success which means more passion. Similarly, in business a natural ability for maths doesn't make you an accountant, but training does. And that training enhances your talent, and you get praised for your work, and so you have the passion to work harder.

A talented team

For businesses, managing and harnessing talent is an enormous challenge. Large, successful businesses need the right combination of talents to succeed, and each talented individual needs to be put in the right role. There's no point having a room of technical geniuses perfecting the latest gadget if there isn't someone on the team who can sell those gadgets. One of the defining factors of successful companies is their ability to deploy talent in the right positions. Good managers and successful entrepreneurs will always talk about how important their team is: they instinctively know when someone is in the wrong job.

The most valuable asset any business has isn't their premises or the product: it's their talent. And that talent walks out of the door every night! When I give a speech, I often find myself asking: 'Do you know who the most valuable people in your organisation are? Do you have a plan to nurture their talent and hold on to their services?' I can assure you that the CEOs of the most successful companies don't let talent get away.

Talent spotting is a key skill. I frequently meet managers and company directors who can tell me all about their own work, but very little about what their staff are up to. I've even been shown round offices and been told 'I don't really know what this department does'! If a manager doesn't know their team, how can they be sure they are employing them to their advantage? Putting the right person in the right job can transform their individual productivity *and* the company's. A good HR department will create a job for talented members of staff, rather than letting good people go, just as a good coach will build a football team around his best players.

Managing data is pretty straightforward, but managing talent requires its own set of skills. Talent usually comes packaged with personality, ego and its own agenda. Many a business has blundered by either letting their talent rise to the top even when the individuals involved didn't have the skills to manage the business – certainly many a football club has made the mistake of handing the manager's job to their star player – or else they underestimate and under-reward the talent. What often happens then is that the talented people quit to set up a rival, rather like the guys who left

Hewlett Packard to launch Apple when HP couldn't see the point of personal computers.

Talent, unlike other resources a company buys in, cannot easily be measured. In football, Cristiano Ronaldo is arguably the greatest player of his generation and a guaranteed goal scorer, but when speculation about where his individual future lay became a distraction to the team ethos at Manchester United, Sir Alex Ferguson was happy for him to be sold (the £80m fee from Real Madrid probably helped). Sometimes talented individuals can overpower a team, and unbalance a business. One of the most talented Manchester United players I've ever seen was George Best. He was a beautiful man who played the beautiful game, well, beautifully. His skill was dazzling and to watch him taking the ball the length of the pitch at Old Trafford was one of the great sights in sport. His talent was unbelievable, but the problem with George was that he knew it. What he needed was a manager who didn't tell him how brilliant he was, but how brilliant he *could* be if he trained harder. If ever there was an example of squandered talent, it's Georgie Best.

Of course, Best didn't just have a talent for football, he had a talent for living. When asked what he had blown his money on, he famously replied: 'Booze, birds and fast cars – the rest I squandered.' Managing a character like Best is a responsibility and a big headache for most organisations, but those organisations that find a way to harness talent are the ones that endure.

Part of the reason we prize talent so highly is precisely that it is mercurial. Just because a golfer won the last Open, it doesn't mean he'll make the cut at the next tournament. The salesman who was last year's highest earner could fail to meet this year's targets. Even the most talented people are rarely consistently talented. How often have we seen a football player bought for millions from one club fail to deliver at his new club? Instead of having a team who are all using their talent and harnessing their passion, when talent is mismanaged, it is squandered.

In sport, there is an acceptance that your talent will diminish with age. As you get older, you accept that you won't have the muscle power or the acceleration you had in your youth; sports people understand that talent ebbs and flows. In business, however, I see a lack of understanding that talent isn't constant. There may not be the steady decline in talent that we see in sport – indeed, in most fields, talent increases with age and experience – but there will always be fluctuations in individuals' ability. Just as a middle-distance runner switches from the 1500m to the 5000m, and eventually to the marathon where willpower can compensate for the physical shortcomings, professionals in business need to be redeployed to make the most of their changing talents. The best companies make sure their best people are employed in roles where they can do their best work. Leaving people to stagnate in roles that no longer challenge them, where their passion for the job slowly ebbs away, is the biggest waste of a resource any company can make.

I often visit companies where I meet a lot of enthusiastic, bright and capable individuals, but the companies they work for aren't making the most of them because they are being poorly deployed. I think this is an area where sport can really teach and inspire business. Think of a football team and how the different skills – not to mention physical builds of players – mean they play in different positions. If you can find a role to match the talent, your players excel at what they do, they grow in confidence and their passion starts to win games.

In the car on the way home from conferences and speaking engagements, I often find myself wondering just how many of the people I have been talking to are 'mis-employed'. The companies – and the teams – that find ways to let individuals use their talent and their passion are, I believe, the ones that will thrive in the long term.

> **Case study**
> Name: Bill Gates
> Business: Co-founder Microsoft
> Years in business: 35

Bill Gates is usually characterised as a nerd. Media profiles frequently sketch a technical genius who finds it easier to relate to technology than people. It's no wonder, then, that the popular perception of him is as someone whose wealth has been built on his prodigious ability to write computer code. If you stopped a hundred people in the street and asked them what they thought Bill Gates's talent was, I bet the majority would say the answer has something to do with computers. But some might tell you that his talent is for business, and I'd have to agree with them.

When it became clear in 1975 that the new computer industry offered greater opportunities than education, Bill Gates dropped out of Harvard to work full time with his friend Paul Allen. Together they wrote software for one of the very first personal computers, the Altair 8800. Gates and Allen called their new business Microsoft, and they achieved modest success for a few years until, in 1980, they had their big break: IBM asked Microsoft to write the operating system for the first IBM PC.

Instead of writing the code from scratch, Gates and Allen found out that a company called Seattle Computer Products had already written an operating system called 86-DOS. They reasoned there was no point in duplicating SCP's code, so instead they negotiated to lease 86-DOS from SCP – for a fee of $25,000 – and then amended it to IBM's specifications. When IBM accepted the renamed MS-DOS, the two young entrepreneurs took the precaution of buying the rights to 86-DOS from SCP for $50k. It must have seemed like a lot of money at the time, but if they hadn't bought those rights, SCP would have been the beneficiary of a huge percentage of Microsoft's sales. I wonder how many other young entrepreneurs would be comfortable making such enormous purchases early on in their career. It seems pretty obvious to me that Gates's talent for business exceeded his programming skills.

Gates and Allen weren't the only geeks fooling around with code and motherboards in the 1970s and early 1980s, yet it was their company that came to dominate the computer industry. This happened not because they were the most talented writers of code, but because Microsoft got its strategy right. Just as less talented athletes can win races because they had the better game plan, Microsoft came to dominance because it got its strategy right.

Some commentators call Bill Gates 'cream cheese' because he seems to have a talent for finding a role for himself between two slices of someone else's bagel: he took a slice of IBM, a slice of 86-DOS and smeared a generous helping of Microsoft on both of them. If you can bear to extend the cream cheese analogy a bit further, you could say that the basis of Microsoft's success has been that their DOS and Windows operating systems sandwich nicely between slices of computer hardware and slices of software programs.

The analogy is actually pretty apt, because individually a plain bagel and a dollop of cream cheese are pretty boring, which means no one will pay that much for either. But when you put them together, you have something much tastier, and therefore much more valuable. Microsoft became an enormous company because it made itself indispensable: before long, both the hardware manufacturers and software developers needed Microsoft. Put simply, without Gates, their businesses were less effective, and less valuable.

MS-DOS did not take over the PC market because it was the best operating system. It came to dominance because Gates implemented a very aggressive marketing strategy. Gates famously once said that 'intellectual property has the shelf life of a banana'; he knew it didn't really matter how good his – or anyone else's –

products were, what mattered was selling as many of those products as he could.

Perhaps it was because another operating system could come along at any moment that Gates was so determined to get Microsoft's DOS tied up with as many computer manufacturers as possible. Alan Sugar remembers the Microsoft rep 'constantly coming back' to his Amstrad offices and refusing to take 'no' for an answer. Eventually Sir Alan saw his chance to negotiate hard on the licence fee he would have to pay and felt that he had got a bargain. But it was Gates who benefited: in a sense it didn't matter how much he sold his operating system for, it only mattered that he sold it.

You don't get to be as successful as Gates, or as dominant as Microsoft, without attracting a fair amount of controversy. Software firms complain that Microsoft has too much power, and customers complain that their products are too expensive or don't work as well as they should. However, I think even his detractors admire Bill Gates, and not just for his well-documented philanthropy.

Gates has been asked many times for the secret of his success, and his answer is that there are actually seven secrets. The first is: *take action*, by which he means, 'Don't just talk about doing it, do it!' Other people could have said, 'Wouldn't it be great if computer manufacturers bought our operating system'; he was the one that went out and sold it to them.

His next secret is also pretty simple: *hire the best people you can find*. Every time you're paying the salary of someone who isn't pulling their weight, not only are you wasting money, but you know your rivals are employing someone you should be hiring. Never stop looking for the best people available. 'At Microsoft there are lots of brilliant ideas,' he has said, 'but the image is that they all come from the top – I'm afraid that's not quite right.' In other words: he has a great team.

Secret number three is this: *know your business*. It was because he understood Microsoft's cream cheese qualities that he was able to make money. He knew what his business did, and he knew what the industry needed. Secret number four is a little harder to achieve: *become the industry standard*. If you can pull it off, you become extremely defensible.

I wonder if his fifth secret is the most important: *work hard*. Gates is one of a number of entrepreneurs who got rid of his TV because he saw it as a distraction from something more significant. He doesn't have a lot of time for religion either: 'In terms of allocation of time resources, religion is not very efficient. There's a lot more I could be doing on a Sunday morning.' The harder you work, his theory goes, the more of an advantage you give yourself. Certainly this is true in sport: the more you train, the better your results.

His sixth 'secret' is also pretty obvious: *sell, sell, sell*. There's no point having the best operating system in the world if you can't sell it . . . because someone with a slightly inferior operating system will always be more motivated to sell theirs.

So far, his secrets have explained how he attained success. His seventh explains how he's retained it: *futurethink*. His golden rule is to make your product obsolete before the market does. It sounds counter-intuitive: after all, if you've got customers who like your product and are paying for your product, why would you take it away from them? Gates's belief is that if you don't improve on your offering, someone else will.

3

SOMETHING TO BELIEVE IN

I knew I would win a gold medal at the Sydney Olympics in 2000. Despite the fact that I had been diagnosed with colitis and, more recently, diabetes; despite the fact that the diabetes had affected my training schedule; despite the fact that the last measurements of my fitness in training had been well below par; despite the pressure of millions of people watching on TV expecting me to win my fifth gold; despite the fact that I was thirty-eight years old – a dinosaur in sporting terms – I still knew we would win.

In sport, belief is frequently the difference between winning and losing. On paper, there wasn't much to separate the six teams that lined up at the start of that final. We had all trained hard, we were all fit, we were the best in our field, and there were three other teams – the Australians and the Italians, as well as the New Zealanders who had won the last international regatta before the Olympics – who would have considered themselves entitled to the gold. But they didn't win, we did.

Sometimes after I give a speech there will be a question-and-answer session, and very often I will be asked about belief: how do you get it, where does it come from, how can you use it? However, I occasionally get the odd person who will stand up and, instead of asking a question, will tell me that their idea for a business or product is so brilliant that the whole world will one day know their name! It's clear that some people have belief, and some people don't – but it's also very apparent that there is a fine line between unshakeable inner faith and delusion.

Imagine for a moment that you're catching up with an old friend and she starts to tell you about her new idea for a business. Perhaps she's decided she's going to set up a chain of clothes shops and that one day there will be a branch on every high street in the country. Do you believe her? It depends: if she's previously worked in fashion retail, you might think it sounds less far-fetched; if she currently already runs a boutique, it might sound even more plausible; if she already runs a couple of boutiques and you know they're making her money hand over fist, then it might even sound probable. However, if she's never worked in retail, let alone fashion, and is so overdrawn she wouldn't get a loan from a bank, then her ambition seems laughable. The kind of belief I'm talking about isn't the delusional kind, it's the variety that springs from experience.

On the starting line in Sydney, I had twenty-five years of race experience behind me. I had won Olympic titles before and I knew what it would take to win another. I had absolute faith in the talent of the other men in the boat and our ability to work as a team because we had already won races together. My belief had very strong foundations.

Belief doesn't always come from experience, however. Some people can conjure it out of thin air. In 2001, Barry Cowan was the 265th best tennis player in the world according to the ATP rankings. He got a wild card into Wimbledon that year and won his first ever match at SW19 to set up a second-round encounter with the world number one, Pete Sampras. The match against Sampras went according to plan, and after a blistering fifty-one minutes the defending champion was two sets up. In the third set, however, something changed: Cowan started to believe in himself.

He held his serve and forced a tie-break. A tie-break

against the world number one, in which a mis-hit might mean you are out of the tournament, requires nerves of steel. But somehow Cowan took his chances and claimed a set off the mighty Sampras. As he powered through the fourth set, he even broke Sampras's serve. Then something truly remarkable happened: the crowd started to believe Cowan could win. Sampras hadn't been beaten at Wimbledon since 1996, but the invincible champion looked like he was going home early.

Barry Cowan had been working with a sports psychologist for the previous few months, and she had encouraged him to connect with his inner belief. Using NLP (Neuro Linguistic Programming) she helped him tap into the aspects of his game that he could believe in. In the opening sets, his timing and accuracy had been great, but his serve had let him down. Cowan focused on the things that were going well and refused to dwell on his serve. The nerves he used to feel on key points were kept under control by imagining success and by recalling previous occasions when he had won matches. Between games, Cowan was seen listening to his Walkman, and when he stepped back out on to the court, he seemed renewed; and Sampras appeared stunned. Cowan later told the press he had been listening to 'You'll Never Walk Alone', the anthem of his beloved Liverpool FC. You could see it in his eyes: he believed he could win. Cowan took the fourth set 6–4.

At the beginning of the fifth set, however, Pete Sampras was a changed man. Just a few games earlier he had been putting shots wide or into the net, but in that fifth set, the champion returned and he quickly surged to a 4–0 lead. His serve was devastating, and Cowan was duly devastated. Sampras won the final set 6–4.

What had happened? I think that Sampras connected with his own reserves of belief. Perhaps he had been guilty of underestimating his opponent, and the two-set cushion made him a little too comfortable, but when he was in danger of losing the match, Sampras had hundreds of career victories to call on for strength. He knew he had the shots, he knew he was fit enough and he believed he would win.

I'm not saying Cowan's belief was a pipe-dream, far from it. Taking the world number one to five sets is a remarkable achievement and testament to how far belief can get you. But when it came down to it, Sampras simply had more to believe in. He was going for a sixth consecutive title to beat Bjorn Borg's record, he had been the world number one for five years, he had completely dominated his sport. He *knew* he could beat the 265th-ranked player in the world.

The foundations of belief

We can all have dreams and ambitions to achieve great things, and there will be days when we all believe we can do remarkable things. Some days that belief will get us out of bed and drive us to achieve success, but enduring success is only secured when our belief is built on solid foundations.

When Duncan Bannatyne, one of the Dragons from *Dragons' Den*, saw an ice cream van for sale, he thought to himself, 'I can do that, I can sell ice cream.' He bought it for £450 and started his first business. Even though he had no previous business experience, he believed he could make a living on the back of a £450 investment. Over the next few years, he built up the business and soon owned a fleet of ice cream vans and was earning a phenomenal salary.

At some point in his career as an ice cream vendor, Bannatyne had the idea to open a care home for the elderly. Unlike the ice cream van, building a care home costs hundreds of thousands of pounds, involves health authority bureaucracy, requires the hiring of specialist nursing staff and finding enough residents to fill the home. But for some reason, even though he had no experience of the care home industry, he said, 'I can do that, I can make money out of that.'

I think this is a really interesting example of the importance of belief. I think most of us would think we could run an ice cream van for profit. We've all bought ice cream, we know what the products are, we can all go to a wholesaler and buy cornets and chocolate flakes, and we can all sit outside a school at home time and find customers. It's *plausible*. If something is plausible, we can believe in it.

Opening a care home, on the other hand, is probably beyond most of us. We'd be utterly daunted by the money involved, the bureaucracy and the commitment; yet to Bannatyne, this was an entirely plausible thing to do. So plausible that he remortgaged his house, sold his ice cream business and his car and took out loans on credit cards to fund the building of his first care home. What gave him this belief? Two things: first, the fact that he had successfully run his ice cream business and learnt about hiring staff, paying VAT and the administration side of business; and the second thing was the profits he calculated a care home would make. He says that he knew how much it cost to build a home, he knew how many members of staff he needed to hire because government regulations stipulated the staff-to-resident ratio, he had a pretty good idea what his overheads would be and he knew how much the income per resident per week would be because this was a government agreed amount. He added up his costs, totted up his income and saw that there was massive profit in it. He says he had absolute *belief* in his numbers. When friends and family told him he was crazy, when builders scratched their chins before giving him a quote and local authority bigwigs with clipboards considered whether or not to give him a licence, he kept faith with his figures. No matter how implausible it was to the people around him, he had an inner belief in his ability to run a business, and an external belief in the profit his new venture would generate.

Perhaps if we had all run a starter business, more of us would believe we could run more complex businesses. Anita Roddick had run a B&B before she started The Body Shop, Rupert Murdoch had owned provincial newspapers before he bought his first national title, and Richard Branson had run a record label before he risked everything to start an airline.

Could Bannatyne have started the care home business – which made him a multimillionaire within five years – without first having run the ice cream business? I wouldn't want to bet against it, but my hunch is that without the ice cream business any future venture would have been hampered by a lack of belief. I don't doubt that the people who stand up in Q&A sessions to tell me their project is a winner, or indeed the people who now stand in front of Duncan Bannatyne on *Dragons' Den* with their sure-fire, million-pound business idea believe what they are saying. But I am also sure that they will have moments of doubt because only experience, only a track record, can quash those doubts.

In Sydney, did I have any doubts? Did my diabetes give me some cause for concern? Maybe. Perhaps I worried that our opponents thought it made me beatable, perhaps I was concerned that it enhanced their belief in their ability to win, but in the end, I had more to believe in. I had done it before and I could do it again. I was in the best boat with the best team.

> The connection between belief and enduring success is to always have something to believe in.

The connection between belief and enduring success is to always have *something* to believe in. Whether it is Duncan Bannatyne's belief in his profit projections, my belief in my ability to win, or Sampras's belief in his serve, at any given moment in your career you need an unshakeable belief in *something*. Just one thing. One thing that you can do with certainty, or that you can do better than anyone else. If you can always tap into that belief, you can keep on going. The things you believe in will change over time, but if there is always something that you know for sure, you're in with a chance.

At the beginning of your career you cannot know for sure that your business will be worth £100m or that you will one day be the CEO, but you can know for sure that you can make those sales calls. And if you can make those calls then you can make your sales, and if you can make the sales, you can make your targets, and if you make your targets . . . you see where I'm going. It's the difference between belief and delusion. At any given point in your career, if you can find the one thing that you believe in wholeheartedly, you give yourself the edge.

Case study
Name: Sir Terry Leahy
Business: CEO Tesco
Years in business: 31

Tesco is simultaneously the nation's most popular shop – it's said that £1 in every £8 spent in Britain goes through Tesco's tills – and its most criticised. While shoppers appreciate Tesco's range and prices, detractors fear it is too powerful and is able to squeeze its suppliers while putting smaller, local shops out of business.

It's not that long ago that Tesco was just the third biggest supermarket in Britain. It is now the third biggest retailer in the world (behind Wal-Mart and Carrefour), and it sells mobile phones, insurance and appliances alongside tins of beans and bags of carrots. The man who has spearheaded the company's phenomenal rise is its CEO, Sir Terry Leahy.

Sir Terry first worked for Tesco as a shelf stacker during his school holidays, and after university (where he studied Management Sciences) he joined their management trainee scheme in 1979. His rise up the pay scale was meteoric: by the age of twenty-five he was the company's marketing manager. He joined the board at the age of thirty-six and became its CEO in 1997 when he was forty.

As marketing manager, Leahy was credited with innovations that saw it become the leading supermarket in the country. He introduced the Club Card, Britain's first supermarket loyalty card, which allowed the company to get to know its customers' shopping habits and needs while simultaneously giving discounts to loyal shoppers. He also introduced the Tesco Value line of products and their Finest range, effectively offering budget, mid-range and high-end customers something in one store instead of three.

As CEO, he has seen the business expand both its convenience Tesco Express outlets and its Tesco Extra hypermarkets, which along with its supermarkets enables Tesco to serve three separate markets. He has also overseen the company's expansion abroad, notably to Asia and Eastern Europe. Since Leahy's appointment to the top job, Tesco's profits have doubled and it's been estimated that he has created a new job in Britain every twenty minutes for the past ten years. It's quite a CV for a kid from a Liverpool council estate.

Leahy is famous for being unflashy. He drives his own car to his office (which is a nondescript building on an industrial estate in Hertfordshire rather than an oak-panelled room in Mayfair), lives in a modest house (for a guy who earns several million a year), watches Everton play from the terraces rather than the Directors' Box, and doesn't accept lucrative offers to sit on boards of other companies so he can concentrate on running Tesco. He's also just as likely to take advice from some-one working on the till in Tesco than he is from someone in their accounts department about what changes need to be made. It's because he's so down to earth that he has been so good at knowing what his customers want. Terry Leahy puts his faith in people.

In fact, he attributes his success to listening to his staff and listening to his customers. When he became CEO, he brought in his old university professor to talk to his senior staff about their work/life balance because he knows that people work better when they feel valued and secure. He has a reputation as a good and fair boss who never loses his temper, or even raises his voice, because he knows it is counter-productive. 'If you find it difficult to accept failure,' Leahy has said, 'then you won't get innovation because employees will be too frightened. I believe a lot in people. I believe a lot in the potential of people. I've never lost that belief that people are capable of incredible things if you give them the confidence and opportunity.'

His belief that the answers lie with his customers and staff rather than with analysts and accountants takes him out of his office and into one of his stores each week, and other senior staff are encouraged to regularly spend a day stacking shelves. 'There are only six levels between me and a check-out assistant,' Leahy has said, and every member of the team gets a chance to move up to the next level. 'There's one bonus scheme for managers, all managers, including me. That's 3,000 managers. Our Save As You Earn scheme is open to the whole business and has created 100,000 shareholders in Tesco – more than any other company,' he says with pride. It's because of his loyalty to Tesco employees that he is troubled by the reputation Tesco has gained for its 'tescopoly' of the supermarket business. 'If you're working hard on the checkout or stacking shelves, why do you want to pick up the newspapers to see someone is saying you're part of a monster?'

Loyalty seems to be the defining characteristic of Leahy. As he said to one journalist: 'I'm quite loyal. One religion, one football team, one wife, one firm.' There aren't many people these days who spend their entire working life at one company and critics say the fact that he has never worked anywhere else makes him blind to Tesco's flaws: Tesco runs through him like letters in a stick of rock. He answers his critics by saying: 'We are successful because we give ordinary people power. We serve them. And they choose. Some people in society don't like that. They like to be the people who decide what's good for the masses.'

Leahy's belief in his staff, his company and his customers has earned him several accolades in addition to the knighthood he received in 2002. He has been the European Businessman of the Year, *Management Today*'s Most Admired Leader and the *Guardian* newspaper has called him the most influential unelected person in Britain. Few would bet that he won't be the recipient of more honours when he steps down in 2011. No doubt there will be more flak too, but I sense it won't deter his successor – another Tesco stalwart Philip Clarke – from pursuing expansion, both in local stores in the UK and internationally.

Having looked at Terry Leahy's career, it seems that he doesn't just believe in his staff and his customers, he actually believes in Tesco. He believes he is running a company for the benefit of his employees and his shoppers, and if he is wrong, he accepts that he will start to lose both. Ultimately, it is a belief in the market system of capitalism. His belief is that if his strategies are right, he'll make money, and if he's wrong, he won't: take care of your staff, take care of your customers, he says, and they will take care of you.

4

OPPORTUNITY KEEPS ON KNOCKING

George Best was one of the greatest football players of all time but he never played on the biggest stage that football offers its stars: the World Cup. Even though he was, in my view, as good as Pelé he never had a chance to try and lift the Cup for his country. He didn't get the *opportunity* because he was born in Northern Ireland, a nation that is too small to produce eleven players of a high enough standard to qualify for the World Cup, let alone win it.

> One of the foundations of enduring success is to recognise an opportunity when it comes your way, and then to have the courage to make the most of it.

Sport is full of examples of people who have missed and seized opportunities, people who have created opportunities and those who have squandered them. One of the foundations of enduring success in life, not just in business or sport, is to recognise an opportunity when it comes your way, and then to have the courage to make the most of it. The story of George Best and the World Cup shows that opportunity is often out of our hands, which is why those of us who are presented with a chance to shine have a duty to make the most of it.

In sport, opportunities for success are marked out on the calendar years in advance. Right now there are teenagers training not for the 2012 Olympics in London, but the 2016 in Rio, and they're probably thinking that their best chance for success will come four years after that when they're older and have more experience under their belts. This Sunday, there will be talent scouts at junior football matches hoping to find players that will be in their prime at the World Cup of 2014, or even 2018. It's because these opportunities only come round every four years that athletes train so hard for them: there's no point reaching your peak in 2011 when the gold medal is on offer a year later.

Unlike sport, life doesn't go in four-year cycles, but it is still possible to look into the future and spot opportunities. In the film industry, for example, release dates of movies are scheduled to coincide with Christmas and the summer holidays because that's when there are more people looking for entertainment. The book industry floods the shelves with 'holiday reads' in the weeks before the majority of people take their summer breaks. If you bring out your movie or your book outside of these windows, the statistics show you miss out on potential sales. Whatever your industry, there are opportunities out there: the trick is spotting them . . . and then capitalising on them. The individuals and the companies with the longest track records have a remarkable ability to do just that.

Recognising an opportunity isn't always straightforward, however. Let me give you an example. What does Bill Gates (the co-founder of Microsoft) have in common with Steve Jobs (the co-founder of Apple) and Bill Joy, Scott McNealy, Vinod Kholsa and Andy Bechtolsheim (the co-founders of Sun Microsystems) *apart* from the fact that they are computer geniuses and billionaires? Answer: they are all the same age, give or take a few months.

What's this got to do with opportunity? In his book *Outliers*, the author Malcolm Gladwell argues that technically minded kids born in 1955 had a fantastic opportunity to become the titans of the new computer industry. Those born earlier than 1955 either chose other scientific careers, or found work in companies like Hewlett Packard and IBM working on big mainframe computers. The kids from 1955 were just finishing college in the mid-1970s when the first personal computers were made. The 1955ers were young enough not to be tied down with kids and mortgages, nor did they have well-paid jobs that they were too scared to leave. In many cases they were still living at home and could take a risk working in their garages for no money to start the businesses we know today. Kids born after 1955 were still at school when the personal computer industry took off. According to Gladwell, being born in 1955 was an opportunity. If you're wondering how you can be more successful, it might be worth examining the opportunities and advantages that your generation has.

All sorts of things can create opportunities and the world's most successful companies have departments geared up to spotting them. Demographic changes, like an ageing population, mean some businesses are now aiming their products and services to an older age group. A change in legislation can also create opportunity (take the recent government grants for home insulation that have seen a boom in that sector), as can the collapse of a rival business or the building of a new road or a change in fashion. Sometimes the opportunities seem small, but the rewards can still be massive.

Capitalising on opportunity

The people I have spoken to for this book, and the people I have met in my career who qualify to be called an 'enduring success' have all been alert to opportunity. Whether it's meeting someone at a conference and realising that they should be working for them, or seeing a 'For Sale' sign on a rundown building and realising its potential, there are some people who see opportunities where others do not.

A lot of my work these days is in mentoring future sporting stars, and when they are about to line up for their first big race, or square up against a bigger, more experienced opponent, they often tell me that they don't stand a chance: they just can't see that there will be any opportunity for victory. So I sit with them and get them to analyse their opponents and find the dips in their performance that they can exploit. The more we talk, the more they find little chinks in their opponents' armour, and they then go into a race or a bout alert to the chance that their opponent has a habit of losing concentration, or getting frustrated or making a slow start. I help them see that opportunities will happen throughout the event and once they are alert to them, they can start to exploit them.

You never know in sport when an opportunity is going to present itself, but you can always make yourself ready to respond. I remember people talking about Gary Lineker being a 'lucky striker' because he scored most of his goals in the six-yard box, tapping in someone else's effort. I used to get a bit cross when I heard that because his effort had been in getting into position. He had made sure that when the cross came in he could get on the end of it. Because he anticipated the opportunity, he could capitalise on it.

In sport, as in life, the more prepared you are, the better chance you have of making sure opportunity doesn't slip through your fingers. Perhaps the best ever example of someone preparing *just in case* they got the right opportunity is Jonny Wilkinson. The England fly-half practised kicking a rugby ball with a dedication that seems almost absurd. In the week before a game he would do 300 place kicks from various points through-out the field. He'd do the same for drop kicks – 250 on the right foot, 250 on the left. He was famous for staying out on the field for hours after his teammates had finished their training session. His dedication meant when he was passed the ball, that pass became an opportunity to score. The opportunity of his career came thirty-five seconds from the final whistle in the World Cup final in 2003. England and Australia were level at 17–17 when Matt Dawson passed to Jonny Wilkinson, and in that instant those hours and hours and hours of preparation meant the opportunity was seized: England became world champions and Jonny became a national hero.

Sport teaches us that if we get ourselves in the game, if we stay alert, we may just get an opportunity. In the 1999 final of the Champions League, Manchester United were down 0–1 to Bayern Munich as the clock registered the start of the ninetieth minute. Most teams would probably have given up at such moments, but United kept pressing their opponents even though many of their supporters had started leaving the stadium. Just as the fourth official announced three minutes of added time, United were awarded a corner. David Beckham curled the ball into the box and it pinballed between the players until Ryan Giggs took a wayward shot on goal, but substitute Teddy Sheringham was in position to steer the ball into Bayern's net. They were – incredibly – level.

As the remaining United supporters cheered, pretty much everyone in the Nou Camp stadium prepared themselves for thirty minutes of extra time and the torment of a 'golden goal'. Everyone, that is, apart from the eleven men on the pitch wearing red. They ran the ball to the centre spot for the restart and almost immediately forced another corner. David Beckham floated the ball in, Teddy Sheringham headed it down and Ole Gunnar Solskjær's foot flicked it into the top corner. In the 92nd minute they had created and capitalised on an opportunity to score. Three minutes earlier the Munich supporters had been celebrating near-certain victory, but now the glory and the title were heading to Manchester.

The best ever lesson sport can offer as a reminder that if you get yourself in the race you might just get the opportunity to win comes from the Winter Olympics of 2002. Five men lined up for the final of 1000m speed skate. Australian Steven Bradbury was off the pace for the entire race, but on the final lap the other four competitors got so close to one another that they collided and all crashed out. A few yards behind, all Bradbury had to do was stay on his feet to claim gold!

Before you start calling him a jammy so-and-so, wait till you hear about how he made it to the final: virtually the same thing happened in the previous race! The other competitors had also crashed in his semi-final allowing him to qualify in first place. Now you're really thinking he's a jammy git.

However, I think he was very smart. Knowing that he was the slowest of the finalists, it was actually his race strategy to sit at the back of the field to see if the same thing happened again. He knew it would be his best chance of a medal. He didn't plan the crash but he *did* plan to capitalise if a crash happened.

If you can't spot the opportunities, then you have to create them. It's one of the reasons I have been so passionate about bringing the Olympic Games to Britain: there is no other event that can inspire and galvanise a generation to achieve more than they otherwise would. The funding for sport has increased as we get closer to 2012, and up and down the country athletes are training that bit harder to make sure they get the opportunity to compete in front of a home crowd.

Of course, the Olympics aren't just an opportunity for the competitors. The tourism industry will see a surge, equipment specialists that serve the outside broadcast industry will probably have a good year, and no doubt people living near the Olympic venues will be able to rent their homes out for a sizeable profit. Because we know when the Olympics will happen, we can make sure – like Gary Lineker – we're in a position to benefit. Hotel owners who want to capitalise on the Olympics will be refurbishing their rooms the winter *before* the Olympics, not during the Games! Broadcast equipment suppliers will be missing a trick if they don't have enough stock to sell or hire out.

If you know how to spot an opportunity and you are prepared for them when they arise, you give yourself the very best chance of securing one success after another. You can't always guarantee that you'll get an opportunity – just ask George Best – but the more you prepare, the more you look, the more the odds are in your favour.

> **Case study**
> Name: Mark McCormack
> Business: IMG sports management
> Years in business: 43

At some point in the late 1950s, Mark McCormack – a Yale law graduate who had nearly been good enough to make it as a professional golfer – must have had an idea.

And that idea must have been something like this: just as many people watch sport as watch movies, so how come sports stars aren't as rich as movie stars? With that idea, Mark McCormack identified a massive opportunity and pretty much single-handedly changed the business of sport for ever.

He had played against Arnold Palmer in amateur tournaments and when they next met he offered to represent him as his agent. In 1959, Heinz had paid Palmer $500 to use his image in a year's worth of ketchup ads. In 1960, McCormack's International Management Group started adding zeros to that figure. By the 1990s, IMG was negotiating $100m-a-year contracts for the world's greatest golfer, Tiger Woods.

McCormack soon represented Gary Player and Jack Nicklaus, which meant the three biggest golfers of their generation all had the same agent. From then on, every important golf tournament would – at some level – involve Mark McCormack. He had spotted the opportunity, and now he had the power to make the most of it because of the incredible clout he had when negotiating contracts. Some people might have been tempted to use strong-arm tactics in such a situation, but by all accounts, Mark never abused this power.

Agents don't always have the best public image. Clients will complain that they take their percentage for very little work, or they persuade their client to do something that's good for this year's profits but bad for the long-term credibility and career. Mark McCormack wasn't that kind of agent. He cared about his clients just as much as he cared that they got paid what they were worth.

I am now represented by IMG, and even though Mark died in 2003, his imprint is still visible throughout the organisation. IMG has thousands of employees in thirty countries and all of them could tell you a story about Mark. One of my favourites is the tale about his relationship with the Royal and Ancient Golf Club (R&A) at St Andrews. Many people wanted to represent the R&A, and like the others, Mark's offers were continually rebuffed. Whereas other people might have walked away, Mark kept going back to them with suggestions for projects until they realised that he really, genuinely cared about the Open Championship. He knew there was an opportunity, and he wasn't going to be easily dissuaded from pursuing it.

Eventually the officials at the R&A agreed to meet Mark to discuss sponsorship for the Open, and he invited them to his house in Florida where they could work in the morning and play golf, of course, in the afternoon. It wasn't until the end of the weekend that the R&A men realised Mark hadn't mentioned his fee.

No doubt slightly suspicious, one of them asked what he would charge. Mark replied: 'Whatever you think is fair.' And he meant it. He trusted them to pay him a fair price, and they in turn trusted him to represent them fairly. He certainly wasn't going to jeopardise a relationship for the sake of a deal. One of his most famous quotes was: 'All things being equal, people will do business with a friend; all things being unequal, people will still do business with a friend.'

Towards the end of the 1960s, Mark started signing some of the world's best tennis players to IMG (including Betsy Nagelsen, whom he married), and from there IMG attracted the biggest stars in every sport, from football to motor racing and – eventually – even rowing. As IMG grew, Mark realised there were other opportunities. In the US, the number of TV channels was starting to grow and they were all hungry for programming. Mark's response was to form a production company – TWI, which still films many of the world's biggest sporting events – and sell the footage to broadcasters. And of course, if an event was going to be televised, there were sponsorship opportunities that weren't going to be missed.

Mark knew how much money event organisers were making from selling TV rights to events, and he realised that he could take a cut for selling those rights, or he could do something radical: he could start his own events and instead of getting a slice of the deal, he could keep all the revenue for IMG. He applied similar logic when he started building sports academies: if he made his money out of representing sports stars, it made sense to train and guide the next generation of sporting greats. It's no wonder that *Sports Illustrated* magazine called Mark 'the most influential man in sport'.

The people who worked with him know why he was able to achieve so much: the man worked hard. Very hard. He would regularly get up at 4 a.m. and be in his office on the east coast of America before his employees in the London office were at their desk. Although he delegated tasks to people around the world, he did not delegate responsibility for those tasks and was able to stay on top by making sure that the things that needed to be done got done.

He was famously organised and was rarely seen without a yellow legal pad on which he made detailed notes. His days were broken down into fifteen-minute slots and he was apparently so busy that he even had to timetable in when to sleep! When he looked at the tasks he had to do each day, he made a point of doing the difficult things first. That way they wouldn't hang over him and drag him down for the rest of the day. He had a similar view in meetings too: if he had something bad to tell you, he wouldn't skirt around it; he'd get it on the table straight away so that whatever it was could be dealt with and both parties would leave the meeting feeling more positive.

There is no doubt in my mind that Mark McCormack changed sport. By spotting opportunities and working hard to get the most out of them, he also changed the lives – and in some cases, the fortunes – of the clients he represented.

5

THE DRIVE TO SUCCEED

When you're a multimillionaire, what drives you to stay in business? Why doesn't everyone sell their business when they're a couple of million quid to the good and go and sip cocktails on the beach? Equally, when you've won an Olympic title, what drives you to defend your title? A lot has been written over the years about what drives people to succeed, but is the drive that gets you to the top the same as the drive that keeps you there?

In boxing, there have been a lot of competitors from poorer nations. It's not so hard to see why a country like Cuba has produced more than its fair share of champions. Unlike, say, a rowing lake which takes millions of dollars to build, a boxing ring can be erected fairly cheaply, and for guys with a bit of talent the ring offers riches and glory not available elsewhere. In Britain, you don't come across many boxers from middle- and upper-class backgrounds: unless something's driving you to perform in the ring, you'll find a less painful way to pay your bills.

My sport, rowing, is typically associated with public schools and Oxford and Cambridge universities. As a kid from a comprehensive school, I was definitely the odd one out. I don't want to compare rowing to getting beaten up by a heavyweight in a boxing ring, but it is still a sport in which you put yourself through agony to win. Your lungs scream and your muscles feel like they're bleeding: yet men and women with university educations choose to put themselves in a boat when they could be doing something else (and that something would pay them an awful lot more than anyone's ever earned from rowing). This tells me that you can't simply explain drive as a consequence of a lack of options.

If we look at the top ten tennis players in the men's game, what separates them? They are all supremely talented, they are all supernaturally fit, they all train for several hours a day. Some have more experience than others, but on any given day at any given tournament, they are all capable of beating each other. So why is it that one of them, Roger Federer – with sixteen grand slam titles (and counting) – has won so many more titles than the rest? Could his drive explain it?

When I examine my own drive to get in a boat every morning, even on the days when it was raining and the icy water would get inside my collar and run down my back, I think I did it for the simple reason that I knew I was good at it. A little bit like those mountain climbers who are compelled to scale dangerous peaks simply because 'they are there', I was compelled to row because I could. It certainly wasn't the lure of fame or fortune. When I started rowing in the 1970s, Britain hadn't won an Olympic rowing gold since the 1940s, and I bet that if you'd stopped a hundred people on any high street in Britain in the 1970s and asked them to name a rower, not one of them could. Clearly, I wasn't rowing for glory, and I certainly wasn't rowing for money (even in my fourth Olympics in 1996, I had to pay to compete).

I don't think you can underestimate how important it is to find something you're good at. I think we all like being good at something, and often the buzz we get from fulfilling our natural aptitudes and abilities drives us on. There are parallels in business too. If you are good at selling, you're going to get a thrill from closing a deal; if you're a fantastic negotiator, you're going to derive pleasure from piecing together a settlement; if you're a technical genius, you're going to feel compelled to find solutions to technical problems. When we find ourselves in situations where our natural talents can thrive, I believe we are driven to achieve.

> " Drive is the element that turns ambition into action. Without it, ambitions are as much use as daydreams. "

Drive is the element that turns ambition into action. Without it, ambitions are as much use as daydreams. Despite this, describing someone as 'driven' is often seen as an insult. In Britain, we aren't very comfortable with people being explicit about their ambition. You can see it when athletes are interviewed on TV. In a pre-race interview, a Brit will often tell the cameras that they just 'want to do their best', whereas an American, for example, will tell an interviewer that they are there to win. I don't think for one second that the Brit wants to win any less, it's just that Brits are more reluctant to be seen as driven.

I think I know why. Driven people are often characterised as single-minded – which is probably true – and that often means that they trample on other people's toes, not to mention their feelings, to get what they want. People often talk about 'blind ambition' where someone is ignorant of the consequences of their actions for the people around them.

There is a subtle difference between ambition and drive. Ambition is the end result, and drive is the desire to see that result come about. If the ambition is a noble one – like winning an Olympic race, for example – then the drive needed to make it a reality comes from a good place. When the ambition is morally dubious, then I can see why some people are uncomfortable with the label 'driven'.

Manufacturing drive

In my experience, drive is the natural result of mixing together the right amount of *vision*, *talent* and *opportunity*. If you have the right vision and if your goals fire you up and inspire you, and you combine this with either a natural aptitude, or a talent acquired through dedication and training, you have the basis for something extremely powerful. When you add the third ingredient of opportunity, then drive happens fairly spontaneously.

Whether you look at Roger Federer or the investor Warren Buffett, you see two men who have both vision and talent, and when they are given the opportunity to win a title or make a fortune, their drive to achieve those outcomes is immense. If I look at my own career, I was fortunate enough to have a natural aptitude for rowing that developed into a talent through training. As I matured as an athlete, I acquired a vision of the competitor I wanted to become, and every four years I was given the opportunity to prove myself on the biggest stage in the sporting world, the Olympic Games. That combination gave me the drive to succeed.

When I retired from rowing, I no longer had those opportunities to compete and my drive waned until I started a charitable foundation with the aim of raising £5m in five years. In 2006 I ran the London marathon and was promised £1.8m in sponsorship. Now I have far less talent as a runner than I do as a rower, but my vision of raising £5m in five years compensated for my shortfall in talent, and of course the opportunity to race at such a public event gave me the drive to achieve.

But there was also something else going on, something that the more I look at entrepreneurs and CEOs, the more I think it might be the fourth magic ingredient of an enduring drive to succeed: fear. I was absolutely terrified of letting people down. The charities that would benefit if I raised the money, my sponsors, the people who were training with me: if I failed, *all* their efforts would be eroded. So even though I had injured my Achilles tendon, I kept on training, and kept on running. Do not underestimate the power of fear. I sometimes wonder if Roger Federer is afraid of who he would be if he stopped winning.

At the time of writing, I am training for another charitable endurance feat. A team of us – Malcolm Cooper, Jonathan and Nick Spencer-Jones, Ian Neville, Pete McConnell, John Mottram and Francis Paxton – are preparing to cycle from the Pacific coast of America to the Atlantic in just eight days. When I was in my twenties, after the 1984 Olympics in Los Angeles, I had a holiday in the States and it took me eight days just to drive across America, and now we're going to cycle it in the same time! Although the money we will raise from this will be less than I achieved for my marathon run, what's interesting is how much easier I am finding it to get to the gym and get out on my bike, even when there has been snow on the ground, than it's been for the past couple of years. All of a sudden I have a goal, and that target has focused my attention. I have four months to get in shape and there's no way I won't be fit enough to cycle across America because I am absolutely terrified of letting people down. Apart from the guys I'll be cycling with, there is our vast support team and our sponsors. And I haven't even mentioned yet that the charity we're raising funds for is Sport Relief. My drive to get fit and arrive on the east coast to see the Atlantic Ocean sparkling in the sunlight is immense.

Sustaining drive

The key to enduring success is finding a way to sustain that drive over the long term. What's the difference between the entrepreneur who grows his business over the decades, and the one who sells it when a decent offer comes his way? Over the years I've wondered whether one of the other elements of drive is ego. Could Federer's ego be driving him to set an unmatchable target of grand slam wins so that his name will always top the table? In business, is the desire to be higher on the annual Rich List than a rival sufficient motivation? Are CEOs driven by the applause they'll get from share-holders at the next AGM? I don't doubt ego – or self-belief as some people would call it – has a role to play, but when I look at the two richest men in the world, I see a distinct lack of ego.

I've never met Bill Gates, the co-founder of Micro-soft, or Warren Buffett, the world's richest investor, but when I've seen both of them interviewed, they don't strike me as being driven by their overweening egos.

Something else is spurring them on and I think it is because they have a vision of who they are and what their companies stand for. They are both endowed with formidable talent and they keep exploiting opportunities for growth. Whether or not they get more opportunities than other business leaders because they're lucky, or because they are better at spotting them, or expert at creating them, I'll explore in a later chapter.

The examples of Buffett and Gates also highlight the difference between the kinds of people who start a company and the kind of executives who are often hired to run them. The drive of a founder to secure the long-term success of the business they started is almost always likely to be stronger than the drive of a hired hand. Corporate executives who topped off their degrees with an MBA or an internship at the right sort of management consultancy or finance company don't, on the whole, mind what company they work for: they mind what *kind* of company they work for. So long as the pay, package and status are sufficiently valuable, many don't care if they are in the oil sector, the hospitality sector or the banking sector. Their drive is personal.

This is a real problem for companies and we've seen, in the past few years, just how big the salaries have become in the banking sector in order to attract the most motivated people. Individual bankers benefited at a time when their employers suffered.

It's not just at the super-rich end of the scale where you find a misalignment between the employee's drive and the objectives of the employer. There are some organisations where there is a culture of protecting individual pensions, or jobsworths doing the bare minimum to ensure they don't get sacked.

The companies that work best are the ones where there is the greatest alignment between personal and corporate drive. It's hard to achieve, but it is something that can underpin long-term success. A smart entrepreneur doesn't take so much money out of his company for himself that his business can't pay its bills. A smart corporation should do the same: personal rewards should be in proportion to corporate gains. That way, the entire team maintains its drive to make sure targets are met, and – of course – bonuses get paid.

Case study

Name: Dame Anita Roddick

Business: The Body Shop

Years in business: 31

In 1989, Anita Roddick attended a gathering of Amazonian tribes who had come together to oppose the building of a dam that would see their homelands flooded. Some were in favour of it, because the developers offered cash, but others were against it. Roddick's solution was to propose an alternative: she offered them a deal that guaranteed to buy their entire harvest of brazil nuts at a price that gave them more money than the developers were offering. The Amazon tribes got an income that was secure for years to come, and Roddick got a supply of brazil nuts that she crushed and turned into moisturisers and conditioners to sell in branches of The Body Shop.

I don't suppose that, when she opened her first shop in 1976 selling lotions and potions she had made at home, Anita Roddick saw herself as a corporate warrior, but that's what she became. Initially her aim was to earn enough money to live on while her husband went travelling, but as The Body Shop grew, so did her awareness of what could be achieved through the commercial sector. She realised that products which were ethically sourced and ethically sold could create real change, and she went all out to bring about as much change as she could.

I was surprised to learn that Roddick once claimed to 'hate the beauty business'. Why then, would she go into the beauty industry? The answer is pure Roddick: because it sold 'unattainable dreams' to its customers who were overwhelmingly female. 'It lies. It cheats. It exploits women,' she said. She wanted to offer an alternative that empowered her customers as well as her suppliers. She wasn't just looking for a business to invest in; she said she wanted 'something to believe in'.

Roddick was one of a number of a new style of entrepreneurs in the UK in the 1970s – Richard Branson was another – who showed us all that anyone could run a business, not just City types in suits. In an era when business was sober and grey, Roddick offered a mouthy, multicoloured alternative. She also showed us that running a successful business was not just about making money. Deals like the brazil nut agreement with the Amazonian tribes meant that The Body Shop cosmetics – unlike 90 per cent of the world's cosmetics – were made with natural ingredients. Her passionate commitment to animal welfare meant that not only did The

Body Shop products not contain animal by-products, they weren't tested on animals either. She was also one of the first retailers to mention recycling.

When her cruelty-free cosmetics readily found a market, she realised she had stumbled across the idea you might call 'ethical consumerism'. She also saw that this gave people a reason to choose her products over her rivals', and that this meant it was possible for business to be an engine for change within society. In the 1970s, the social responsibility of employers usually extended no further than providing a subsidised canteen and paying for the Christmas party. Wider social problems were seen as belonging to the realm of charities. Roddick thought differently and once claimed there 'is no more powerful institution in society than business'. She told a charity she supported that the day of the bring-and-buy sale was over and it was time for the economy to effect real and lasting change. Her drive to bring about this change was unstoppable.

When her husband Gordon returned from his travels, he became an integral part of the business, taking care of the paperwork so that Anita could focus on product development. After opening a second shop in Brighton, the Roddicks decided the best way to grow the business was through a franchise operation. However, even this was conducted unconventionally.

Instead of charging start-up fees, which is how most franchisors make their money, Anita Roddick personally interviewed all the candidates (who were predominantly the kind of women who had been her customers) and is reported to have selected them on the basis of how they answered questions like 'what's your favourite flower' and 'how would you like to die'? She was determined that the people who would become advocates for The Body Shop had to share its values. Most businesses are measured by their financial results; Roddick saw this as a particularly unimaginative way of assessing a company's worth.

Roddick was a trailblazer for the fair trade movement, something I have become involved in over the past few years. I too have learnt that when companies make the right ethical choices, their customers are more likely to choose their products. My clothing brand FiveG was struggling a few years ago. It was breaking even, but it was taking up too much of my time for it not to return a profit. It was only when my partner in the business, an extremely astute guy named Alok Ruia, suggested that we used fair trade cotton for our clothes that FiveG really took off. I have since visited some of the farms in Africa and India we buy cotton from and can understand why Roddick was so passionate about fair trade: it makes *such* a difference. I now know what

Roddick knew: fair trade changes lives. And it only costs a few extra pennies a product to do it.

It was Roddick's refusal to put profit first that once led her to say: 'I'm not a good businesswoman – most entrepreneurs aren't. We're delinquents. Everything these days is to do with economics – people speak as if you were put on this earth to keep the economy going. I'm here to be a good mother, wonderful friend and an activist. End of story.'

It was because of statements like this that her customers were bemused – many said they felt let down – when Anita and Gordon Roddick sold The Body Shop in 2006 to L'Oréal, a traditional cosmetics company with a history of animal testing and using chemicals in their products. Roddick, who became Dame Anita in 2003, assured her customers she would not have done such a deal if she had not been convinced of L'Oréal's commitment to retain The Body Shop's ethical credentials. She hoped that The Body Shop's example would prove to its new owner that to be ethical and profitable were not mutually exclusive.

Roddick was not one for compromise. 'I wake up every morning thinking . . . this is my last day,' she once said. 'And I jam everything into it. There's no time for mediocrity. This is no damned dress rehearsal.' These words took on new potency when she announced in

2007 that she had been diagnosed with hepatitis C. She received outpatient treatment, but the long-term prognosis was that she would need a liver transplant. However, she did not live long enough to receive it. In September 2007 she was admitted to hospital complaining of a severe headache and died the following day of an acute brain haemorrhage. It was a very sudden death for a woman whose drive had seemed indefatigable.

6

BE PREPARED ... FOR ANYTHING

In the run-up to the 2008 Olympic Games in Beijing, I was asked to help out behind the scenes with the British women's rowing team. The women's quad were world champions and joint favourites to win, so apart from encouragement I wasn't too sure what sort of help they needed as they were doing pretty well without me. I started off by asking them about their race plan, and I was given a document that set out – practically stroke by stroke – how they were going to approach the race.

'This is great,' I said, 'It's really thorough. But what if you're not ahead after 250m? What happens then?'

They had no plan B.

> " The plans that simply state what you're going to do are of limited use; the ones that explain how you're going to do it are much, much more valuable. "

I've been involved in a couple of charitable ventures where people have said things like: 'We'll start on this project in September when we've raised the money.' It's been down to me to ask the obvious question: 'What if we don't raise the money?' There's a very big difference between planning and preparation, and in my experience planning to succeed and *preparing* to succeed produce remarkably different results. Good race plans and good business plans have a lot in common: the plans that simply state *what* you're going to do are of limited use; the ones that explain *how* you're going to do it are much, much more valuable.

Our race plan for the Olympic final in Sydney was a very detailed affair. The length of the first ten strokes were decided, as was our strike rate for the first 500m, the second 500m, the third and the fourth. If there was a headwind, we anticipated a slightly lower strike rate: earlier in my career I might have felt the need to stick to my strike rate no matter what, but experience had taught me the importance of responding to conditions.

In athletics, the most advantageous position to be in is at the shoulder of the lead runner; that way you don't expend unnecessary energy setting the pace and you can respond if anyone goes past you. In rowing, however, the best place to be is to lead from the front: we sit backwards in the boat, so if you are in front you can see what the opposition is doing. In pretty much every race it was always my plan to get into the lead and stay there, but of course the other teams had their own ideas and my *plan* didn't always pan out. However, I was *prepared* to find myself behind. In the weeks leading up to the race in Sydney, the four of us and our coach Jurgen Gröbler discussed every possible eventuality. What happens if the Australians get ahead of us? We reasoned that they would have had to put in a superhuman effort to do that which meant they would probably tire. If it happened, we knew we wouldn't panic. Together, the five of us talked through every option and when we lined up at the start of the race we were prepared for everything.

Preparing for pressure

One of the reasons it's always a good idea to have an experienced member on any team is that they can prepare for pressure. If you've never competed in an Olympic final, you don't know how you will handle the pressure. If someone in the boat knows not just what it's like to compete, but what it takes to win, then that's a distinct advantage. Sometimes, however, the experience of losing can increase the pressure. Instead of recalling positive memories of your last big tournament, you panic that you are about to make the same mistakes again. Which is why I always tell young athletes competing in their first major final that they have absolutely nothing to lose and no baggage to hinder their preparation.

At the 2010 Winter Olympics in Vancouver, the Canadian Melissa Hollingsworth was the favourite to win the women's skeleton. Britain had two competitors in the race that sees sliders go head first on 'skeleton' sledges at 90mph down the bobsleigh run: Shelley Rudman, who hoped to go one better than the silver she had won four years previously; and Amy Williams who had never previously won a title on the world tour. It was an absolutely thrilling competition, in part because it didn't go to plan. Rudman, desperate to prove she was capable of gold, probably tried too hard on her first run and never really got to grips with the track: she didn't get her race plan right and ended up towards the back of the field. Although she performed better on the second day, it was too late to recover. Hollingsworth, on the other hand, put herself in contention with a series of excellent runs, but it was the outsider Williams who broke the course record and led the event from the start.

In the skeleton, the competitor with the fastest accumulated times from the previous rounds competes last. In the final round, Williams was in the lead and Hollingsworth – the home favourite – was a few tenths of a second behind. Hollingsworth's was the penultimate run: all she needed to do was go a bit faster and hope that the inexperienced Williams bottled it on her final run. Instead, it was Hollingsworth who felt the pressure. The entire nation was willing her to succeed. She was desperate to live up to her billing as the favourite and she went all out for gold. Her blistering speed came at the expense of accuracy, and she ricocheted off the walls, slowing her down so much she ended out of the medals. As she burst into tears of frustration and disappointment, Williams prepared to start her final run.

The inexperienced Brit got her slide off to a good start and put in an excellent run. When she got to the bottom, her coach was there to greet her. 'How did I do?' she asked, seemingly oblivious to her race time. 'You're Olympic champion,' he said. When I spoke to her half an hour after her victory, she asked me how long it would take to sink in. 'It probably never will,' I told her.

The reason I'm detailing this race is because it shows how important it is to prepare for every aspect of a race. Winning the skeleton didn't come down to taking each corner perfectly, it came down to nerves. Williams dealt with hers, Hollingsworth didn't. It didn't matter what was in the Canadian's race plan, because she wasn't prepared for how it would feel to have your entire nation expecting you to win. It's a lesson I hope British competitors in the 2012 games learn from.

If you've ever watched *Dragons' Den*, you'll have seen entrepreneurs stand in front of the Dragons and start their pitch for investment, and while some of them are brilliant and convincing, others dry up. Or they stutter. Or they make inappropriate jokes. You can see the sweat pour off them. They are clearly absolutely terrified. My hunch is that they spent too much time preparing what they would say, but not how they would say it. I absolutely know how they feel: the first time I was asked to do some public speaking was when I was twenty-two. I had just returned from my first Olympics with a gold medal around my neck and I was taken on an open-top bus tour of my home town. The guy organising the event told me at the outset that when we got to the town hall, I would have to make a speech. I was so petrified that I couldn't enjoy my time on the bus waving to crowds who seemed genuinely happy for me. All I could think of was the prospect of making a speech. If I had known further in advance, I could have prepared for it.

My preparation wouldn't have just been about what I would say – that was pretty straightforward, all I had to do was thank my family, coach, back-up team and the local community for supporting me – it would have involved controlling my nerves and, if I stumbled, how I would get myself back on track. My preparation would have been that detailed.

Business plans

When people start new businesses, they are usually advised to write a business plan that sets out what their business does and how it will make money. Much of writing a business plan is, frankly, guesswork: 'I think we'll sell this many widgets', 'I think we can produce the widgets for £1 and I also think we can sell them for

£5'. Once a few basic assumptions about the mechanics of the business have been articulated, much of the rest of the document is extrapolation: e.g. 'if we hire five people to sell the widgets we multiply our sales by five and our turnover increases accordingly'.

While these business plans can help you visualise a positive future – and I've already said how important vision is – they don't always help you anticipate what lies ahead. Good business plans make you really think about what it takes to bring about a certain outcome and forces you to think logically about how to sequence events to get the maximum benefit. But even those business plans assume that everything will eventually work out for the best.

What happens if widgets cost more to manufacture than you thought? What happens if a rival widget seller comes to town? Or if your widgets are found to be faulty? Or if a change in the law means people don't need widgets any more? Business plans that anticipate the widest range of outcomes are the most valuable. As a CEO, you need to know how you will respond if your sales figures are down or if a rival goes bust. And if things go better than expected, how would you spend the increased revenue? On a Ferrari, or more staff?

I learnt a very useful lesson about preparation when I went into the clothing business. Shortly after the Sydney Olympics, I was approached by a clothing manufacturer to see if I wanted to endorse a new range of socks. At the time, I thought I would only have a short period of time to capitalise, financially, on the profile the fifth gold had given me and so I told my agent to set up a meeting. When I met the team from the Ruia Group I really liked them, and the initial idea evolved into designing and launching a new range of cotton menswear. We launched with a modest selection of shirts, fleeces and trousers under the FiveG brand. All our clothing had one thing in common: I would be happy to wear them. The thinking was that if I liked them, there was a pretty good chance that other men would like the clothes too.

Under the leadership of Vimal Ruia, the Ruia Group had a great track record in the cotton industry (they're one of the biggest manufacturers and importers of cotton goods in the country), so I was quite happy for them to take the lead when it came to ordering stock or devising the marketing campaign. After all, at this stage I had only stopped rowing a few months previously and my track record in business did not compete with theirs. Not long after we got the first samples back from the manufacturers the Ruia Group decided to take out some adverts in the Sunday supplements, confident that we would get some interest.

The ads were pretty successful – just as we had hoped. In fact they were too successful and we were inundated with orders. However, we hadn't prepared properly. We quickly ran out of stock and couldn't fulfil all the orders. Also we based our sizing on me. Being quite a big person I class myself as being extra large. Having my own frustrations at not being able to get clothing to fit, I thought this was a great solution. However, some of the customers who had received their orders realised the clothing that they had ordered wasn't to the sizing they expected and returned their purchases. Our planning – which had been along the lines of design garments, get garments made, place adverts, sell garments – was faultless but our preparation hadn't been good enough. If only I had applied what I had learnt from racing to business!

The fact that FiveG is now very successful and, nine years on, branching into womenswear is proof that we learnt from our mistakes, and there are plenty more stories from FiveG's evolution I want to share later in this book. Needless to say, we are now prepared for pretty much anything.

The more I learn about business, the more I see the importance of mastering the art of preparation for attaining and maintaining success. Large corporations have entire divisions preparing their next moves. So if a rival launches a new product, they'll have prepared to drop the price of their product. Or if the cost of oil rises above $150 a barrel, they will implement their plan to invest in green technologies. Whatever the problem, they'll have a strategy prepared. Some of the big software companies even keep a few billion in cash, just in case a rival they didn't anticipate launches a game-changing piece of software. That cash isn't to replicate what their new rival has launched or to increase their own marketing budget – it's to buy the new rival. The bigger the organisation, the more intricate the preparation.

No matter what you do, the better your preparation, the better your results.

Case study
Name: Warren Buffett
Business: Berkshire Hathaway investment
Years in business: 54

Warren Buffett is the world's most successful investor. He started his investment partnership in the 1950s investing his own money and that of friends and family in the stock market. In his first decade, he returned an average of 30 per cent a year, and it's been calculated that if you had invested $10,000 with Buffett in 1965, it would now be worth over $50m. By comparison, the same amount invested in a fund that tracked the Standard & Poor 500 Index would now be worth $500,000.

With a track record like that, perhaps it's not surprising that at various points over the past ten years, Warren Buffett has been the holder of the title of 'the world's richest man'. Even less surprising is the level of interest that people have in learning his investment strategies. My own research tells me that the basis of his success is preparation.

In an industry where most people talk about making a gain or a loss at the end of the day, or make decisions based on quarterly accounts, Buffett is known for taking the long view. 'If you won't be happy owning a stock for ten years, don't buy it,' he has said.

While other investors work in the fevered atmosphere of a Wall Street or City of London office with flashing computer screens and constant phone ringing, Buffett works in a small office with a handful of staff in Omaha, Nebraska. He doesn't have 'power lunches' with clients or rivals which means he doesn't get caught up in the hype that controls so much of stock market movements. He is geographically and emotionally detached from that environment, and this seems to enable him to make smarter decisions.

Buffett's preparation is legendary, and he's been very open about sharing his techniques and the secrets of his success. Anyone with his patience can, in theory, repeat what he has done, and hopefully repeat his success. Be warned though, you need a lot of time on your hands.

The main criterion Buffett looks for is undervalued stock. This makes sense, but determining the true value of a company, as opposed to its stock market valuation, takes time and skill. Buffett spends months analysing a company's books before he comes to a decision, and only if his valuation is at least 25 per cent above the market's valuation will he invest.

The next thing he examines is what a shareholder's return would have been over the previous decade. Other investors are happy to look at last year's dividends, but Buffett looks at the long-term trend. This can tell him if the business is consistently well managed, and this is one of his investment criteria.

Buffett's thorough analysis of a company's valuation also involves assessing its level of debt. His view is that profits become vulnerable and erratic when a company has to make onerous loan repayments: if interest rates go up, the company may end up in the red. The next thing he examines is the profit margin. Again, unlike other investors who might look at last year's profits, he looks at the past five years' profits and makes his own calculations of the real profit (not the profit the company's accountants will have claimed). If the profit margin is large enough, and if it shows a steady increase, he'll be more likely to invest. Pretty obviously, this means Buffett doesn't generally invest in new companies whose valuations are more susceptible to hype. By picking 'boring' stocks, he can better gauge the real value of a company.

He likes companies he invests in to be defensible, which means that they either have to offer something unique that cannot easily be replicated by a rival, or they have to be so dominant in an industry that it dissuades others from competing against them, which was the case when he invested in Gillette and Coca-Cola. Of course, this criterion means his preparation takes even longer, as he also has to investigate rivals to assess how much of a threat they present.

His last investment tenet also seems thoroughly sensible: don't invest in anything you don't understand. No matter how much research he could do into dot-coms or tech companies, Buffett knew he would never understand what they did so he would be unable to assess their value. Many people considered him 'past it' when he declined to make any dot-com investments, but when the dot-com bubble burst we were all reminded why Buffett is known as 'the sage of Omaha'.

The result of this thorough preparation, then, is that Buffett has the confidence to make a decision he will be able to stick to. Which is just as well, because he bets big. Once his methodical preparation has identified the stock he should buy, he buys millions of dollars of shares in that company. His philosophy – unlike most investors – is not to diversify because that inevitably means that some of the stock you're holding is going to be second best. If you've identified the best, he argues, you should invest in the best.

I suppose what I get from looking at Buffett is the realisation that detailed, intense and focused preparation can – odd as it sounds – make complicated things seem quite straightforward. He has his values and his vision which guide him, but it is his preparation that enables him to make effective decisions.

As well as his phenomenal, unrivalled track record in investment, Buffett is also known for his down-to-earth attitude to life. He lives in a modest home (just the one) and is known for his simple tastes. He clearly has more money (his wealth is estimated around the $40bn mark) than he can ever spend, which explains why he is also one of the world's leading philanthropists. In 2006 he announced that he was giving the bulk of his wealth to charity. The charity he chose was the

Bill and Melinda Gates Foundation run by the Microsoft founder and his wife.

There aren't many people who give substantial sums to charity without wanting to put their name either on a foundation, or at least the foundation stone of a hospital or school. Anyone giving the amount Buffett is giving – an estimated $31bn – might demand that entire towns were named after him, but Buffett appears to have a complete lack of ego. His reasoning was that the Gates Foundation had the expertise to make sure the money was spent on the right projects. What he was really saying was that Bill Gates had done the preparation.

7

DEDICATION'S WHAT YOU NEED

People of a certain age will recall the kids' TV show *Record Breakers*. Each week, presenter Roy Castle would interview athletes who had broken world records or kids who had swum the Channel, while twins Norris and Ross McWhirter would keep their stopwatches to hand as contestants tried to set new records. Perhaps the most memorable thing about *Record Breakers* was its theme tune. Sung by Castle, the lyrics told impressionable viewers: 'if you want to be the best, and you want to beat the rest, dedication's what you need'.

> " Your willingness to work through the monotonous tasks is an attribute that separates dreams from achievements. "

Dedication is just as important in business as it is in sport. The ability to dedicate yourself to your goals to the exclusion of other – often more exciting – things, and your willingness to work through the monotonous tasks are attributes that separate dreams from achievements. Dedication may not be all you need, but make no mistake, it is an absolutely essential ingredient of enduring success.

Behind every successful meeting, every best-selling product, every client acquisition, and every gold medal, you will find a long period of dedication. We all know that great snooker players practise a perfect 147 break every day; we can see that sprinters get their muscles from somewhere; and we instinctively know that successful new businesses and products aren't launched on a whim; yet it comes as a shock when we learn what really goes into achieving excellence. I'm often asked how many hours training I used to do. 'In a boat, or in the gym?' I would ask.

Rowing is particularly hungry for dedication and

DEDICATION'S WHAT YOU NEED

will gobble up every hour you give it. You don't just need strong arms – everyone thinks rowing is an upper body sport – you also need strong legs to power through the strokes and a strong back to transfer that power from your legs to your arms. You don't just need to do strength training, you need to do endurance work too because there's no point being able to race hard for five minutes if you lose it in the sixth. And of course, your strength and fitness is of little use to you if you don't have the technique, or the race sense, or the water sense.

To succeed in one area of your life, it's almost always the case that every other area of your life suffers. Athletes are constantly making sacrifices for their sport: jockeys and gymnasts spend their lives hungry; tennis players live out of a suitcase; athletes leave friends and family behind to move nearer their training facilities; and no matter what sport you do, you will always find yourself leaving parties early, sober enough to drive home. And that's on the rare occasion that you actually accept an invite. Behind every success, there is a sacrifice.

If you read the autobiographies of anyone who has started a business, you will find stories about entrepreneurs working eighteen-hour days and seven-day weeks for months and months at a stretch. While people focus on their new business, their health can suffer, their relationships can suffer, and there are entire periods of their lives when they couldn't tell you which film won the Best Picture Oscar, or which party won the election, or who won *The X Factor*. All their energy, all their focus, is directed towards one single purpose.

In my career, the fact that there was no money to be made in rowing meant that I had to do all sorts of things outside of training and competing that I would really rather not have done. I took jobs that weren't very much fun, or that didn't pay very well, because they gave me the flexibility to train and compete. After my first Olympic gold medal in 1984, I received a modest sponsorship deal from Leyland DAF, the truck manu-facturer. There was no obvious synergy between trucks and rowing, but Leyland DAF had a plant near my home town and they were keen to support a local athlete. As well as getting their logo on my tracksuit and on my boat, it was part of the deal that I would go to their motor fairs.

I've already said that I was pretty shy back then and the thought of public speaking was almost painful, but all they wanted me to do was take my medal to the motor shows and be around to talk to potential partners. I didn't know what to expect, but I soon learnt that most people only wanted to hear the answer to one particular question: 'So how does it feel to win an Olympic gold medal?' Some days I would be on my feet for hours and would shake hundreds of hands, but by and large the people I met were genuinely curious and supportive, even though very few had heard of me. I can't imagine I helped Leyland DAF sell more trucks, but no other manufacturer had a gold medallist on their stand.

I was so competitive in those days that I hated the days when I couldn't train, and although I was growing in confidence in public, going to motor shows really wasn't what I wanted to be doing. So I told myself that shaking hands at motor shows was now part of my job, just as much as going to the gym or devising race plans. Being dedicated to my sport now meant being loyal to my sponsor. After all, they were paying my rent!

The basics of dedication

Making yourself carry out tasks you would really rather not do takes dedication. Even if you started out enjoying something, when you do it every day for eighteen hours, it's pretty easy to get bored with it, and when you get bored, pretty soon you also get resentful. I have found that there are four elements to dedication, and if you can recognise those components, you can manufacture dedication when it might otherwise ebb away. The first of those components is *choice*.

When you are forced to do something, it usually breeds resentment. When you are ploughing down the river as it's getting dark and it's so cold no amount of exercise will warm your feet; or when you're still at your desk at 11 p.m. and too busy to eat the pizza you had delivered at 9 p.m.; or when you make your thirtieth sales call of the day after twenty-nine rejections, remembering that it is your choice to do those things can renew your dedication to carry them out. You tell yourself that if you really wanted to you could walk away: there might be consequences, serious consequences, but you *could*. There will be aspects of any pursuit that you won't enjoy, but by reminding yourself that *you* are the one pushing yourself to achieve, it becomes more bearable simply because you are in control.

The second component is *discipline*. Somehow you have to make yourself do things you would really rather not, or make yourself do them to a level you just don't have the energy for. So what if you only deliver 1,200 leaflets rather than 1,500 to advertise your new venture? What difference will it really make? When you are not disciplined, it's tempting – and easy – to cut corners, and when you do that, success is not going to be the outcome.

So how do you discipline yourself? The first thing to

do is examine why you're having difficulty – is it the boredom of the task, the length of time it will take to reap the reward, or the time it takes to do it properly? If you can identify the reason why you're being sapped of motivation, you can begin to deal with it. Often recognising the problem is enough as you can tell yourself: 'I know this is going to be boring today, I just have to get through it.'

There are a number of simple techniques that can help you become more disciplined. An obvious one is to demarcate your day, allocating specific times for specific jobs. It's very easy to be distracted by things like email, the web and phone calls, so why not make a habit of dealing with these things in timetabled chunks rather than whenever they happen to arrive? Another simple technique is making a 'not to do' list. The 'to do' list is something we are all familiar with, but a 'not to do' list can be just as helpful: I will not surf the web, I will not go to the pub, I will not go out for lunch. Of course, the best-known technique for instilling a bit of discipline is the 'carrot and the stick'. If you can reward yourself for a job well done or for meeting your targets, and punish yourself for not doing those things, then this can really focus the mind. If you get your work done, you can have that doughnut/pint/hour in front of the TV; and if you don't, you can't!

The next element of dedication is *pride*. If you are pursuing what you might call a 'noble purpose', whether it's to be the best athlete you can be, to represent your country, to make your parents proud or to earn enough money to take care of your family, you can derive a sense of pride from your work. Even on the days when you don't get results, you can take pride in progress, or in duty, or – when things are really bad – in just getting out of bed.

Sometimes it's possible to find pleasure in the effort it takes to carry out a task. There were many times when I was training when I would suddenly find I was incrementally more in time with my teammates, or when my oar caught the water at an incrementally better angle and simply being good at what I was doing – even though I was often in considerable pain – gave me pleasure. Sometimes pleasure is too much to ask for, but when you are ploughing through paperwork or pushing your body that bit harder in the gym, you can usually find a sense of purpose. Pleasure and purpose can enhance and foster a feeling of pride.

The final component of dedication is *focus*, and it can be harder to find than you might think. When you are running a business, especially if you are new to it, you will find yourself doing umpteen different things in one day. You might be making sales calls, hiring staff, paying the phone bill, negotiating an IT contract and so on. Maintaining your focus can be very difficult in situations like that, just as it can be tough to say 'no' when friends invite you to watch the football or join them for a drink.

It's generally true in life that the better you want to be at something, the more you have to focus on it. At GCSE level, students usually do eight or nine subjects; at A level, they study two or three; and for a degree, they focus on a single subject for three years. Focusing on one area to the exclusion of others is the only way to get the expertise and knowledge that underpin success.

It's absolutely vital that people who want to be successful evolve the ability to shut out distractions. Imagine how many choices CEOs of large companies have to make every day. Perhaps their rival is about to bring out a new product and they have to decide if they should bring forward the release of their own product. Perhaps the Budget has just altered their tax liabilities and they need to decide if some of their operations need to be moved into tax havens. Or should they change tack because they've just heard a very persuasive speech at a conference? If they can't maintain their focus, they will be pulled in so many directions at once that they'd never be able to make progress.

Focus means not worrying too much about what the

competition is doing. It means letting some areas of your life slide. It can also mean carrying on with something in the face of opposition. More than anything, though, focus means carrying on with something until you get it right. No matter how boring it is, how hard it is or how long it takes, the ability to see things through to the end is the characteristic that marks you out for success. Whether it's a string of half-finished projects or a week of sub-standard training sessions, failing to see things through to the very end leads to an accumulation of underperformance.

This probably explains why so many successful people are called 'single-minded' in polite company, and 'rude' and 'selfish' when they're not in the room. I know in my own career I've had to turn down invites and even family holidays because of my dedication to my sport. Maybe I lost a few friends because of it and perhaps people even thought I was rude, I don't know. There are certainly experiences I sacrificed so that I could dedicate myself to my sport, but my record of achievement means I am comfortable with the choices I made. If I had not dedicated myself to rowing in the way that I did, I don't suppose I would have competed, and won, at the highest level for so long.

Case study
Organisation: Comic Relief charity
Years in operation: 25

I am asked to get involved in a lot of charity work – it's one of the great privileges of having a public profile – and I sit on the board of Comic Relief and am on the steering group of its sister charity Sport Relief. I see first hand how the organisation raises and distributes funds, and am dedicated to helping the charity do more for those in need. It is a remarkable organisation that has raised over half a billion pounds in the past twenty-five years, which has enabled us to help thousands of projects around the world and improve the lives of hundreds of thousands of people. Comic Relief has also entertained audiences of millions with its spectacular nights on TV. However, what really makes Comic Relief remarkable is the dedication of the people who run it.

Comic Relief was set up by the scriptwriter Richard Curtis in 1985 in response to the Ethiopian famine that had also inspired Band Aid and Live Aid. If musicians could help, Curtis thought, then comedians could do so too. The first Red Nose Day in 1988 saw people do ridiculous things to raise money and they were rewarded with a night of extremely silly television on the BBC. The relationship with the BBC has endured, and the organisation now produces a telethon a year alternating between Sport Relief and Comic Relief.

The annual TV exposure allows Comic Relief to inspire the nation to get involved, and it also means that some of the biggest names in sport and entertainment want to be involved. Remember Tony Blair telling Catherine Tate's Lauren that he wasn't bovvered? Or Ali G interviewing Posh and Becks? Or Hugh Grant kissing Dawn French? Richard Curtis has amazing powers of persuasion and gets people to do all sorts of things they wouldn't dream of doing for anyone else. Sport Relief once persuaded my wife to let the team from *Top Gear* landscape our garden (I don't know if they let the *Ground Force* team race round in sports cars that day, but they couldn't have done more damage than Clarkson and co.). After they trashed the place it took me a very long time to see the funny side. Knowing that it had helped raise money for such a good cause was just about the only thing that made it all right.

I am currently training to take part in one of the world's most gruelling cycle rides. Along with seven others, I will be pedalling from one coast of America to the other and in the process I hope to raise thousands of pounds for Sport Relief. When I'm out fundraising with sponsors, it is fantastic to be able to say to people that every single penny they give will go to good causes. The public know about Comic Relief's commitment to transparent spending, and it's a pledge we are all dedicated to maintaining. We are able to say this to donors because our operating costs – Comic Relief has a staff of about eighty – are met by corporate sponsors, commercial deals (like the selling of red noses in supermarkets, or the *Robbie the Reindeer* books) as well as money from government (which includes the Gift Aid money we reclaim from the Revenue) and interest we earn on bank deposits. This kind of transparent funding makes it easier for our fundraisers to collect money for us.

My commitment to Sport Relief does not normally take up more than one day a month of my time. Richard Curtis – who could do plenty of other exciting things with his time like direct movies, write more scripts, or just spend more time with his family – is completely dedicated to Comic Relief. It is his dedication that has seen the organisation grow from something that was pretty amateur in its early days into one of the most effective fundraising organisations in the country.

Richard may be the public face of Comic Relief, but behind the scenes the man in charge is Kevin Cahill CBE, the charity's unassuming chief executive. He joined the charity in 1991 and has been instrumental in its success ever since. Kevin was responsible for launching Sport Relief in 2002 because he wanted to reach the kind of fundraisers who would rather run for money than sit in a bath of beans. He has negotiated tie-ins with *Big Brother*, *Fame Academy* and *Strictly Come Dancing* that have kept the charity's profile high. And under Kevin's leadership, new technology has been embraced so that people can now text a donation, or pay online, rather than ring up and pledge or pay in person at a bank. He's made it pretty impossible to ignore Comic Relief, which is why 93 per cent of the population has heard of us, and over half of the nation has made a donation.

The money raised by Comic Relief is distributed to projects in Africa and the UK. Comic Relief doesn't run these projects itself because we don't have the same expertise as people on the ground who know exactly how the money needs to be spent. This means that Comic Relief can concentrate on what it does best, which is raising funds, and the imaginative ways in which people raise money for us is one of the many reasons why the words 'compassion fatigue' don't feature in our meetings.

The team is constantly inspired by the feats people perform to raise money, whether it's David Walliams swimming the English Channel, or a class of school-children donating their lunch money, the determination and commitment shown by fundraisers ensures that everyone at Comic Relief feels a responsibility to make sure that money is put to best use. In turn, that responsibility ensures their ongoing dedication. Some days, working for an organisation like Comic Relief, where you are confronted by the effects of poverty on a daily basis, can be hard to take. However, seeing the difference that money raised by people running a mile in their slippers, or all the other ridiculous ways people find to attract sponsorship, means that everyone in the organisation is dedicated to raising even more money in the future.

People who work for Comic Relief can see just how much good the charity is doing. When I am training for my bike ride, when the hill in front of me feels steeper and longer than it looks, I only have to think of some of the projects I have seen during my work with Sport Relief to find the strength to get myself to the top.

Comic Relief is a remarkable organisation with dedicated people working for it, and it is because of the dedication of people like Richard and Kevin that hundreds of thousands of people's lives are improved every year.

8

THE SWOT ANALYSIS

One of the basic components of any business studies qualification is the SWOT analysis, where you assess your Strengths, Weaknesses, Opportunities and Threats. We do the same in sport. If you can exploit your strengths, minimise your weaknesses, seize opportunities and neutralise threats, not only do you make the most of your own talent, you also get the most out of every situation you find yourself in.

> Enduring success relies on finding where your less obvious strengths lie.

To look at me, you'd think it was pretty obvious where my strength as an oarsman lay: in my size. But if you look at the men I competed against, you'll see that being tall and muscular isn't much of an advantage because most rowers have pretty similar physiques. If you look at the commercial world, say at the computing industry, most computers share the same basic functions. If you're selecting a computer on the basis of memory, processing power or operating system, there's not a lot of difference between them. The strengths that took you into your field, whether sporting or commercial, are usually the strengths that took your rivals into that field too. Enduring success relies on finding where your less obvious strengths lie.

I found that one of my less obvious strengths was my ability to intimidate opponents with my record of success. I remember when I won my second Olympic gold with Andy Holmes in 1988, the competition were a little in awe both of our physique – we were two of the strongest competitors at the Games – *and* our success at previous world championships: we were seen as unbeatable and that put us at a psychological advantage. Towards the end of my career, one of the advantages I had was my experience. The simple fact that I had won races before gave me the edge over the other competitors because I knew what it took to win.

I felt the unbeatable reputation of the British crew was so important to our continued success, that I never wanted to give the opposition any reason to doubt it: one failure and we would lose that advantage for ever. In fact I was so sure in the ability of our demeanour to win races that I probably went a bit overboard in my criticism of James Cracknell twelve years later in the run-up to the Sydney Games when he dyed his hair red: I felt we shouldn't give the opposition any reason to think we weren't entirely serious about what we were doing. Looking like a wally, which is what I think I called James, lowered our stature. You see the same situation in commerce all the time: certain companies are seen as invincible. Their reputations mean others are afraid to go into competition against them.

When you get used to winning, there's a very real chance that you underestimate the opposition. It was my assessment that this was potentially my biggest weakness and in the decade that I competed with Matthew Pinsent in the pair, we didn't train to win, we trained not to lose. Matt and I dominated the pair during our career together and we knew that the rest of the teams weren't just training to win, they were training very specifically to beat us. When the margin of victory is often less than a second, we knew that we only had to be fractionally below our best and one of several other teams had to be fractionally better than we had estimated for us to lose a race.

Matt and I never stopped analysing our performance, and that analysis kept throwing up seemingly tiny things that made a difference. For instance, at the end of a practice session our coach Jurgen Gröbler would say something like: 'Really great, guys, you're really making progress,' or perhaps: 'That wasn't so good today, you really weren't trying.' Depending on the feedback we got, Matt and I would head to the dressing room in completely different moods from each other. We realised that Matt responded really well to encouraging feedback whereas I was spurred on by negative feedback. It took us years to figure this out, but once we had we were stronger: knowing what made us feel dejected meant that dejection was lessened. The better we felt, the more we believed in ourselves, and the more we believed in ourselves, the more determined we were to prove ourselves. It's such a small weakness to have identified, but in elite sport, as in big business, the margin between gold and silver can be very tiny indeed.

Dealing with weaknesses

Really successful companies will know their strengths and weaknesses and hire their teams accordingly. I continue to be surprised how many directors and CEOs confess that, like me, they are dyslexic, or aren't very good at maths. Knowing that you find reading a report or analysing a spreadsheet difficult means that you know you need to hire people who are very good at doing those things. Now that dyslexia is much more likely to be spotted at school, it's also much more likely that people will enter the workforce not only *knowing* that they have this weakness, but also *knowing how* to compensate for it by using specialist software programs. Knowing that you have dyslexia helps you to deal with it. If you haven't spotted your weaknesses, you can't deal with them.

My dyslexia is one of the reasons I employ an assistant who makes my appointments, deals with media and charity requests and ensures my tickets have arrived before I leave for the airport. I suppose, at a push, I am capable of doing a lot of those things myself, but the fact is I'm not as organised as she is. I find it hard to say no to requests. I also know that if I booked my own appointments I would also need to develop the ability to be in two places at once! Having an assistant allows me to get on with the things I'm good at.

Of course, not everyone is in the position to hire people who complement their own skills, but they can still delegate tasks they're not very good at to people who are better at them. Most of us accept that we need a trained mechanic to look after our cars, or an accountant to do our tax returns, and whenever we employ experts to do tasks we are not suited to, you generally find that the benefits outweigh the costs because work is carried out to a higher standard and, in all probability, done more quickly than we could do it ourselves. After all, why should someone who's good at sales, or marketing, or product development, also be good at DIY or book-keeping? If I think of all the successful people I know, they all have one thing in common – you never find them wasting time on tasks they're no good at. They've recognised their weaknesses and have developed strategies to compensate.

The SWOT analysis is on every business studies curriculum because it's so effective. Unless you take the time to work out your strengths and weaknesses, as well as the opportunities and threats, you risk missing out on success. In sport, it is possibly easier to see the opportunities for winning than it is in business. Sporting governing bodies announce the dates of major tournaments years in advance, and the events in the annual calendar rarely shift by more than a few days each year.

However, when Matthew and I did our own SWOT analysis, we discovered there were many more opportunities to win than there were races. Let me explain: whenever we turned up at training camps, we made sure we looked confident. If we were carrying aches and pains, we made sure we didn't let anyone else know. And when we gave interviews to the press, we could use them to send out messages of confidence to our opposition.

I see a very clear parallel between our tactics out of the water and some of the most successful names in business. There are some leaders who will do anything to promote their business. Richard Branson even tried to go round the world in a balloon! Some will deliberately grant interview requests to coincide with their rival's new launch or big announcement. Others, like Charles Saatchi, make a deliberate point of never giving interviews knowing that silence can lend him a mystery that unsettles his rivals.

The fact that I trained myself to spot opportunity in sport now filters through into every area of my life. When I retired from sport after the Sydney Olympics, I sat down with my wife Ann – and afterwards my agent – and talked about what on earth I could do for a living. I didn't have any qualifications and I didn't have any great ambition to go and get a 'proper' job. While I know Ann would have liked me to have been around to help out with the house and the kids in ways I never did while I was competing, we both recognised that the publicity surrounding my fifth gold was an opportunity to earn money.

In the days of my Leyland DAF sponsorship I got paid £200 to spend all day shaking hands at motor shows; now I was being offered appearance fees of thousands of pounds to turn up at an event to hand out an award or give a speech. By the time I arrived home from Australia, there were already several offers. Even though all I really wanted was to take some time off and spend it with my family, we could both see that there was an opportunity that needed to be exploited. If I took time off, interest in my success would inevitably dwindle, and so would the offers. In the end I accepted endorsements that, in hindsight, I probably should have turned down.

If we planned things particularly well, there were days when I could fit in two or three personal appearances. Having struggled for money in a sport where there are no financial rewards – I even had to pay to compete in the Atlanta Olympics when I was going for my fourth medal – Ann and I weren't about to walk away from that kind of opportunity.

Capitalising on opportunity

Really successful people know how to capitalise on opportunity. If they've just been featured favourably in their industry trade paper, they'll approach a head hunter to let it be known they might be open to offers. If their company has produced good figures, they'll be the one to announce it; if the figures are bad, they'll let someone else make the statement. If the growth is forecast to come from emerging markets, they'll volunteer to move to the Delhi office.

When we call someone 'opportunistic' we often mean it disparagingly, and when someone is consistently opportunistic, we might dismiss their ability to have always been in the right place at the right time as 'luck'. We do this because it makes us feel better about our own shortcomings and we kid ourselves that we 'could have been somebody' if we'd just had the opportunities that successful people have had. But in doing this we seriously undervalue the skill it takes to spot an opportunity and the courage it often takes to exploit it.

When most people look at the threats on their radar they tend to look at what damage their rivals can do to them. But a trainer preparing a boxer for a fight won't just say: 'He's got a really big right hook, keep your guard up,'; he'll also say: 'Remember he gets tired quickly, just wear him down.' By analysing the threats your rivals pose, you also uncover opportunities. If you can't compete with a rival on price, perhaps you can win on quality or service or ethics. Working out other competitors' areas of excellence can guide you to focus your efforts on different areas.

Of course, there is a problem with the SWOT analysis that people often overlook: things change. Opportunities and threats constantly shift, as do your strengths and weaknesses. Performing a SWOT analysis brings success; performing a SWOT analysis regularly brings enduring success.

Case study
Business: Jaguar cars
Years in business: 88

I should confess straight away that I drive a Jaguar and I love it. Throughout my childhood I looked at Jaguar cars and thought: 'One day . . .' That day finally came when I returned home from Sydney with my fifth Olympic gold medal in my bag. Waiting for me outside Terminal 4 at Heathrow was a beautiful Jaguar XJR. I thought my agent had arranged for it to be there as a 'well done' treat to take me home in, but my wife Ann handed me the keys. It was mine.

It's very easy for me to explain why I always coveted Jaguar cars: they combine a sporting pedigree with gorgeous design, and they are British. As a twelve-year-old, Jaguars were the stand-out car for me. I always wanted to own an XJS, which was the new model at the time, and I actually started to put spare pennies in a six-pint whisky bottle in the hope that I could save up for one. I still have the bottle now. It's never been emptied, but thirty-six years later I've nearly filled it. The contents would probably buy me a windscreen wiper!

There are other prestige motor companies, but in my opinion the designs of Mercedes or BMW or Audi just don't have the curves or the class of a Jaguar. Obviously I'm biased, but I notice that while people can walk past a top-of-the-range Merc in the street, there's something about a Jag that makes people want to stop and touch it.

The company was founded by William Lyons in the 1920s. Lyons thought that cars 'would appeal to a lot of people if they had a more luxurious and attractive body', and started designing cars that would fit on top of an Austin Seven chassis. His cars looked like more expensive models, but were less than half their price. In 1935, Lyons wanted a name for a new model, something sleek that conveyed powerful agility, and the

Jaguar brand was born. From then, good design has been the hallmark of Jaguar.

In the 1940s, Jaguar introduced the XK120, a car that was called the 'sports car that had everything'. Sleeker than anything the company had produced before, it was a road car that looked like it could win a Grand Prix. In the 1950s, the company built on its reputation for speed and moved into racing cars. It dominated at Le Mans throughout the decade.

In the 1960s, Jaguar brought out possibly the most gorgeous car of all time (that's not just my opinion, it topped the *Telegraph*'s all-time poll in 2008): the E-Type. With its huge bonnet and rolling curves it became the archetype for almost every sports car that followed. In the 1970s, Jaguar launched the XJS – the car that had captured my interest when I was a kid – and it seemed to me that Jaguar's position as the nation's favourite car manufacturer was unassailable.

However, in the 1980s Jaguar learnt that good design wasn't enough as the German manufacturers Mercedes, Audi and in particular BMW started to eat away at their market share. During the early 1980s, Jaguar expanded rapidly in the biggest market in the world – North America – and this in turn lead to some quality issues. It didn't help that two of TV's shadiest characters – *Minder*'s Arthur Daley and *Coronation Street*'s Mike

Baldwin – were seen driving Jags and the car's image changed from being associated with sports performance to something, frankly, a bit naff. Jaguar had clearly not performed a SWOT analysis and hadn't anticipated the threat from the German manufacturers.

At the end of the 1980s, Jaguar was sold to the Ford Motor Company and in the next decade the new owners reassessed the brand's strengths and weaknesses. For international buyers, the big draw of Jaguar was seen to be its 'Britishness' and they developed the Jaguar S-Type, a gorgeous-looking car with an old-fashioned grille and more curves than Marilyn Monroe. It was very Inspector Morse (who incidentally drove a MKII). The trouble was that if you're going to spend a year's salary on a car, you probably wanted to feel like James Bond. Jaguar's great strength – its design – wasn't enough.

The engineers and designers needed to produce something special to restore Jaguar's reputation. While there were people like me who had always had a weak spot for a Jag, falling sales meant that they had to win over more than the old die-hards if the brand was going to survive.

In 2007, Jaguar launched the XF series and it finally looked to me that they had done their SWOT analysis. The design of the XF was clearly a Jaguar, but under the bonnet they had learnt a thing or two from the

Germans and I reckon they got some of their ideas for the interior from NASA – it was that impressive. Their weakness – a reputation for underperformance and faults – had been engineered away, and the brand's great design strength had produced the company's first car for the twenty-first century.

The XF also addressed one of the inherent problems with the luxury car market: the kind of driver who can afford to buy one might like to see themselves as a Bond-type, but the chances are that they've got a family and need a boot that can take a lot of shopping. Jaguar saw an opportunity that addressed both the dreams and realities of potential customers: the XF was a four-door saloon with the feel of a sports car. This was a car you could drive on your own and feel like you were chasing bad guys in, *and* it was a car you could fit the family into.

Unsurprisingly, the XF has been a huge success and the biggest threat the model faces isn't from BMW or Mercedes, it is complacency. Jaguar made a mistake when it thought the company's history was enough to secure its future. So long as the new owners, the Indian motor group Tata, ensure that new Jaguar models are developed by addressing their weaknesses as well as their strengths, the Big Cat should be purring for decades to come.

9

LET'S WORK TOGETHER

What's the one thing all the people I've profiled in this book have in common? While some will have been blessed with larger-than-average doses of vision, or been more diligent than others with their preparation, the single factor that they have all benefited from to an astonishing degree is that they have worked with brilliant teams. It's not a coincidence. Although Bill Gates, Richard Branson and Anita Roddick remained figureheads for their organisations, the idea that they achieved their success alone is preposterous.

What's really interesting is that if you changed the personnel in their organisations, I'd be willing to bet that each of the people in this book would still have been ridiculously successful. Why? Because they would have simply found different people and built their teams in a different way. No one can achieve enduring success on their own.

> 66 Teamwork isn't just about surrounding yourself with brilliant people, it's about putting the right people into the right positions. 99

When good teams work together they achieve more as a group than any of the individuals in that team could achieve if they worked in isolation. When bad teams work together, they pull each other in opposite directions, contradict each other and undermine their colleagues. Teamwork isn't just about surrounding yourself with brilliant people, it's about putting the right people into the right positions. If you can do that, a team's value is greater than the sum of its constituent parts.

If you ever doubt the impact teamwork can have you only have to look at the nation's favourite sport – football. When a team isn't doing well, the fans don't chant for the strikers or the defenders to be sacked (well, not often), it's the manager they want out. And sometimes, a new manager comes in and gets radically better results almost instantly. The players didn't suddenly became more talented: the new manager simply got them playing better as a team. I say 'simply', but of course team work is anything but simple. There's been a lot of research done into why some teams work better than others, and psychologists have come up with 'personality types' that make up the ideal team. However, in my experience there have been times when teams that are good on paper don't get the anticipated results. Why? Because teamwork isn't just about getting the right people together, it's about getting them to work together effectively.

I have been incredibly fortunate in my career to have been selected to play a part in the best teams in my sport. The vast majority of my medals, and certainly all my Olympic medals, have been won as part of a team, and over the years, I have had many opportunities to work out why some teams work and others do not.

The first element of teamwork is about respect. In the last chapter I talked about recognising your own strengths and weaknesses; teamwork is about respecting your co-workers' abilities. Nobody is brilliant at everything but the best teams have someone in them who excels in one particular area. Some people are good at coming up with ideas, others are great at implementing them. Some people are great at managing people, others are fantastic at managing data.

Human beings have an unhelpful tendency to admire their own talents above everyone else's, which is why we need to make a special effort to identify our teammates' talents. When I'm watching *Match of the Day*, I always know that when Alan Shearer is asked for his thoughts on a game, he'll more often than not talk about what the strikers did and didn't do. When Martin Keown chips in, his focus is more often than not on the defenders. If you played in a certain position at school, you just can't help yourself from focusing on what the player in 'your' shirt is doing. Good team players make sure they don't fall into the trap of focusing on individual performances; they only care what the group achieves as a whole.

The best teams are what I would call 'frictionless'. The skills are so well distributed among the team that each member makes their contribution without stepping on the toes of anyone else. Tasks happen without duplication and every member works to the best of their abilities. In reality, skills are distributed less than evenly, which means particularly talented individuals have to have their wings clipped so as not to overshadow or overtake their teammates. It can be hard to do this if you find yourself working with people whose skills don't match your own; it is particularly hard if the person leading the team is the one whose skills are deficient. However, being part of a successful team means making yourself fit into the role you've been given. It's only when people know – and accept – their role within the team that it starts to function without friction.

Team building

The best way to reduce friction in teams is to put people into positions that they are naturally suited to. There's no point having a really outgoing person working in the back office with boring bits of data while a shy person is manning the phones and putting in sales calls. Some types of people will always be better at some types of roles. Fitting the right role to the right worker can transform a team's achievements.

The problem with defining roles for particular individuals is that very often there are roles within a team that appear more exciting or more valuable. In our corporate culture we have a tendency to admire the people who shout the loudest, but the fact is that every single role performed by each member of the team is just as important. Without everyone's contributions, the overall success of the team would be diminished.

Sometimes, for the good of the team, you have to accept a role that might not have been your first choice.

For instance, before I started up my partnership with Matthew Pinsent I was paired up with Simon Beresford for two seasons. We had both competed at the Seoul Olympics, but we both rowed on the same side of the boat: stroke side. Fairly obviously, if you are rowing in a pair, you need to have an oar on each side. One of us was going to have to change the way we rowed. At that point, I was a double Olympic gold medallist and he was yet to win a medal. If one of us was going to have to relearn his rowing technique, there might have been an assumption that it should be Simon. In the end, it made sense for me to row on the other side of the boat. I took this as a new challenge, not just to row with a new partner, but to row on the other side. Nobody in the world of rowing had won an Olympic gold medal rowing on different sides of the boat. And I thought this would enhance the team as well. Both of us were taking on new roles. To me, it didn't matter about our individual performances, only about our success as a team.

When Matt and I decided to compete in a four for the Sydney Olympics we knew there was always a risk that the media would talk about the team as the 'Redgrave four'. Even Matt, who was rowing for his third successive gold (a phenomenal achievement by any athlete) was overshadowed by my attempt to win a fifth. We knew we needed to find teammates who would not be intimidated by our record and who would not feel unequal to us. I hated it when the press wrote about the 'Redgrave four' as it was so disrespectful of the effort the other three guys – Matt, James Cracknell and Tim Foster – put in, not to mention their talent and determination.

James and Tim were the perfect foil for Matt and me. If you look at the photo of the four of us on the rostrum (which, by the way, we made sure had Matt and I at either end so the press couldn't crop James and Tim out of the picture) you'll see that they are both physically smaller than me and Matt. The fact that Tim was the smallest of the four might have led some to speculate that he was the weakest man in the boat, but he was probably the best technical rower in the country at the time and we all had to work hard to be as good as him. James's greatest asset was, you could argue, also his greatest liability: his personality. I have never met any-one quite as driven as James and the thing that drove him was fear. Fear of failure. No matter how well train-ing went, no matter how many races we won, James was never satisfied and this spurred us all on. Matt was quite simply a powerhouse, bigger and stronger than the rest of us and capable of driving the boat through the water. I added experience and race sense: I had competed so many times in my career that I could read a race so accurately I would know within a few strokes of the start if we were doing enough to win.

The great thing about the Sydney four is that we all respected each other's ability. We saw how hard each other worked in training, and the time we spent together in the gym and travelling to regattas made us friends for life. And that is one of the things that separates good teams from great teams: fun. Respecting your teammates is essential; you don't have to like them, but if you do, if you would rather do anything than let them down, then you have a group of people that is capable of exceeding their individual potential.

Chemistry

What's interesting to me about the Sydney team is that it almost wasn't made up of the four of us. In the year before the most important race of his life, Tim – for reasons known only to himself – put his fist through a window and did some pretty major damage to his hand. He had to miss a lot of training, and Ed Coode took his place in the boat. Our training with Ed went brilliantly. He is another formidable rower, and was just as worthy of a place in the Olympic team as the rest of us.

However, as there were only four seats in the boat, when Tim was fit again, a choice had to be made. None of us could be sure of our place. On paper we all deserved to go to Sydney.

As I say, sometimes putting a great team together cannot be done with pen and paper; sometimes you can only judge a team on instinct, and there was a feeling that we were just that bit better with Tim rather than Ed. It was an incredibly tough decision but it was one we all stood by because we all trusted the man who made it: our coach Jurgen Gröbler. So far I've talked about the 'Sydney Four' but there's no doubt that there were five of us on the team (and to say that isn't to ignore the countless others – the medics, the trainers, the administrators – who shared our goal and helped us achieve it). Good teams need good leaders and in Jurgen we had someone we trusted and respected. I'll come on to leadership in more detail later in the book, but like the best leaders, Jurgen had the ability to see things in each of us that we were blind to and his skill was to bring our hidden capabilities into the open. I think there are many business leaders who could learn from sporting coaches: good leadership is not about giving orders, it's about knowing and understanding what your team is capable of and then enabling them to achieve it.

Since I retired from rowing I have found myself

working in another team of five. One of the businesses I have devoted my time to in the past decade has been Juice Doctor, a fruit drink for everyday hydration – not really the sports market, but for consumers who take hydration seriously. There were a few so-called 'isotonic' drinks on the market that claimed to replace fluids during or after a workout, but they were all full of sugar (and sometimes also salt). The guys behind Juice Doctor wanted to create a drink that did the same job at replacing the fluids and salts lost during everyday activity, but they also wanted to make it entirely natural. Juice Doctor's selling point was that it was made solely from fruit juices and water. Our target market was going to be people who cared what they put into their system.

The approach from Juice Doctor came at a time when I was getting a lot of offers to endorse products. I was being offered five-figure sums for personal appearances but the Juice Doctor team weren't offering to pay me anything. I was nevertheless really interested to hear more about their idea and their potential business. It wasn't just because I believed in the product – which I'll discuss in more detail in Chapter 16 where I tackle the subject of setbacks – it was because I believed in the team.

Of the four-man team one had experience of the supermarket business and knew how to get products into stores, two had financial management expertise and the fourth was an actor. You might wonder why I thought an actor was so valuable to a soft drink operation, but TJ is the epitome of a 'people person': we needed someone who could go out and sell the juices and TJ was the kind of guy you'd buy anything from. But the great thing about the people at Juice Doctor was that they had recognised their strengths and weaknesses and they had realised that they needed a fifth person, someone whose name could open doors and who had credibility in the market. I could see they needed someone like me too, and knowing that I genuinely added to the sum of their parts was the reason I got involved. I was more than happy to take my fee out of future earnings because I felt that between us we had what it took to make Juice Doctor a success.

For me to get involved in a new venture, whether it's Juice Doctor, the FiveG clothing brand or a charity, I don't just look at the individual product or campaign, I look at the team. If you can find yourself part of a team where the individuals' talents complement each other, where you are inspired by the same goal and where you can achieve more together than you can apart, you are pretty much guaranteed to enjoy your work. And the more you enjoy something, the longer you'll be wanting to do it.

The back-up team

There is, of course, another team in my life without whom I would not have achieved very much: my family. My parents and my sisters have always supported me, doing far more for me than turning up to cheer me on at races. My parents never questioned my odd choice of career and never pressurised me to get a 'proper job'. My mum even trained as a driving instructor to earn more money to help provide the funds I needed to compete.

Throughout my marriage, my wife Ann has shown the kind of understanding that only another rower could have had for the life that I chose, and even now I've retired, she continues to understand that my work takes me away from home, which leaves her with the lion's share of the household chores. My support network has been absolutely central to my success.

I have been incredibly lucky. Some people are surrounded by people that undermine their ambition, or who make too many demands on their time. The more you are able to surround yourself with a team of supportive friends and family the easier it is to find the courage to take action. If friends or family are less than supportive, then it's important to find that support from elsewhere. Sir Jackie Stewart is an advocate of having a mentor, someone you can turn to for feedback or advice when you are unsure of the correct course of action. He himself had two important mentors in his career, King Hussein of Jordan, who became a friend because of his passion for motor racing, and Lord King, the former chairman of British Airways. 'I think their contribution to my success is immense,' he told me. 'They had no [financial] interest in any of my businesses and I knew they were impartial. They only ever offered a genuine opinion and never told me something because they thought it was what I wanted to hear.' It was precisely because these two men did not work for Sir Jackie's businesses that they were such a vital part of 'team Jackie'. I am sure that Sir Jackie was as valuable to them as they were to him, and that's why his friendship with his mentors can be measured in decades not years.

Your teammates might not be immediately obvious. They might not necessarily work in the same office as you, or on the same project as you, but when you find people who are brilliant at what they do, and whose skills complement yours, don't let them get away. Successful people like Sir Jackie are always putting new teams together, and are always looking for people to make up those teams. In sport, we have structures for talent spotting and employ people to act as scouts. It's another area where business could learn from sport:

sometimes you have to go out looking for the talent you need to complete your team.

Case study
Name: Barbara Cassani
Business: Former CEO Go Airlines, Chair of the 2012 bid
Years in business: 26

In 2003, I received a phone call from a fast-talking American woman who wanted to talk to me about bringing the Olympic Games to London. I knew that, as a country, we had decided that we were going to bid and were on the longlist of nine countries bidding for 2012, but no one had been appointed to put a team and a bid together. Barbara was phoning to say that she had got the job, and a couple of days later she was sitting in my kitchen and persuading me to join the bid team.

Within a few months, the team had grown to thirty or forty people all with different priorities. There were people from the Mayor's office, people from the local boroughs within London, from various sports governing bodies and from the Department for Culture, Media and Sport. It had the makings of a complete mess, but Barbara's extraordinary leadership skills kept us on track. She was able to do the business equivalent of herding cats and somehow got us all working as a team.

Barbara Cassani's background was conventionally corporate. She had spent a few years at Coopers & Lybrand before rising through the ranks at British Airways and launching Go Airlines. Her career had clearly taught her how to bring people together. 'My job is often to focus everybody on one objective and keep reminding them what it is as we work towards it,' she says. By offering clarity, she gets her teams moving in the same direction.

Barbara's unusual in that she has combined a fairly traditional corporate career with entrepreneurial get-up-and-go, which is presumably why BA asked her to launch their low-cost subsidiary. Go Airlines was a success, Barbara believes, because of the team she was able to hire.

'We chose people for specific roles,' she remembers, 'we didn't hire people who we thought could develop into the role. So often you see companies hire people they like and then find a role for them; we didn't do that. We also hired team players. We interviewed some very strong candidates, but we had to pass on them because we felt they might be disruptive.' Once her launch team was in place, she was then very clear about how everyone would work with one another. 'In a lot of organisations, one of the easiest ways to manage yourself in a meeting is to throw the blame on to other people and to try to deflect away from what's wrong with your department; I simply didn't accept that behaviour; it just wasn't acceptable to rag on colleagues in meetings. When people made mistakes – which are inevitable in a start-up – people weren't hauled over the coals or fired. We all discussed how we could make things better.' Her message was clear: we are a team, we work together and we succeed or fail together.

From talking to Barbara, it is clear that what made the difference at Go wasn't that people were *made* to work as a team, they *wanted* to. 'It was my view that my personal behaviour and that of the people at the top of the organisation was more powerful, and would set the tone more effectively, than any document we could have written on our "corporate culture". We completely stripped out corporate speak or MBA language so that there wouldn't be a divide between the people in leadership positions and those delivering services on the front line. There wasn't a Christmas party for the cabin crew and another for the people in suits, we were all together. I wanted everyone to feel like it was *their* airline.'

When the company had a problem, everyone on the team was involved in coming up with the solution. 'I didn't want the company to go into blame mode; I wanted us to be in solution mode. I think when you're honest with people, they're honest back. For instance, we had a problem with cabin crew sickness. When you have a rate of sickness at 15 per cent, then you have to hire a lot more cabin crew and pilots than you do if your sickness is 5–6 per cent, which is normal for airlines. So when our rate started to creep up, we sat down with everyone and said: "What do you think we should do?" No one had ever been asked for their opinion before!

'They told us that they thought some people weren't really sick, that they were probably hungover or just taking time off instead of using their annual leave. So I levelled with them and explained how much it was costing us, and between us we devised a solution that meant if people were sick more than twice in a certain period, we could call them and ask if everything was OK. It didn't go on their record, it wasn't disciplinary, it was just a call to see if people were OK, because flying around all day isn't for some people.

'What happened was amazing. The sickness rate came down in part because some people realised they shouldn't be flying – it's a tough life – and the people who had been pulling a "sicky" stopped, simply because it would have been too embarrassing to sit there and pretend they'd been sick.'

After British Airways sold Go to easyJet, Barbara brought her teamwork skills to the 2012 bid. 'To start with it was just me and my mobile phone and I got quite a lot of phone calls from different branches of the government saying: "We've got this person who is spare so we're going to send them over and you can use them." I had to say: "No, I don't want spare people. I'd rather it stays just me and my mobile than take your deadweights." I think it was the best decision I ever made, and it was quite frightening at the time, but I think not being British helped because I hadn't grown up with that deference for those institutions. I'm not sure if I could have said no to the Senate or the White House in the same way.'

Barbara was allowed to build her own team in her own way, and her choices were vindicated when the London bid was included in the shortlist for the 2012 Olympics. It was at this point that I – along with a lot of other people – realised just how important teamwork was to Barbara. 'To this day, people believe that I was forced out but I wasn't,' she says. 'In my view good leaders make sure they've got the right people in place. It was my determination that once we were into the final round, the bid needed a different leader. I think having an American in charge was confusing, so I went to the government and told them that they should hire

Seb Coe. They were reluctant, presumably because he had been a Conservative MP, but I took them through my logic and they realised it made sense.'

Not many leaders step down of their own free will, and fewer do so because they have realised – and are willing to admit – that there is someone better to take on the job. But Barbara knows that no leader can be better than the team they lead, and no team can achieve its best without the right leader.

10

GATHERING MOMENTUM

Nothing breeds success like success. Nothing prepares you for a good finish like a good start.

It makes sense if you think about it. Let's say you want to get some stationery printed. How are you going to go about doing that? In all likelihood you'll ask around for a recommendation for a good printer, and when you get that recommendation you'll probably use that printer. The printer that was successful enough to be recommended becomes more successful through recommendation. No matter what walk of life you're in, a little bit of success often opens the door to a little bit more success.

Winning is a habit. The fact that I won my first Olympic gold medal at the relatively young age of twenty-two definitely contributed to my future Olympic victories. Not only did the first win teach me what it took to win gold, but it gave me the belief that I could do it again. It also – and I don't think anyone can quantify how valuable this is – made my competitors believe I could win again.

In Premier League football where teams play one or two matches a week, the effect of momentum can more easily be seen. Take Arsenal and the 2004/5 season. The previous season they had been dubbed 'the Invincibles' after remaining unbeaten for all their thirty-eight matches. They were only the second club in history to have been undefeated in the top flight of English football for an entire season, and watching them, it was easy to see why. Even as a Chelsea fan, I couldn't help but admire – and occasionally enjoy – their beautiful passing play. They oozed confidence and they tried set pieces that most teams wouldn't dare simply because they believed they could pull it off. Winning had become a habit. Meanwhile, every team that prepared to play them was probably guilty of thinking: 'If we can get a draw . . .' or, 'If we don't lose by much . . .'

It was always going to take a strong team to stop them, and I suppose it is inevitable that that team would be Manchester United. Fairly early on in the 2004/5 season, they beat their London rivals 2–1.

Arsenal's incredible undefeated run of forty-nine matches had come to an end. For the next couple of games, Arsenal struggled. Same players, same manager, different attitude. A couple of draws followed, an easy win against a lowly opponent, a scrappy win: their season didn't fall apart (they actually finished second that year) but their game did. The spell had been broken. They knew they weren't invincible any more, and so did every team who played them.

Of course, it's not just winning that can become a habit. Losing can too. I sometimes wonder if the career of my friend Ben Hunt-Davis might have been different if he had had a major win early on in his career. Ben was one of the best junior rowers of his generation, and I got to know him because we used the same training facilities. He had so much promise as a rower that he dropped out of university to concentrate on his sport. He spent the next eight years not winning medals, sometimes not even getting into the final of major championships, but he just kept on going.

Knowing that he was good enough to win gold spurred him on and he was determined that when the next major competition came round he would be in the crew. He finally made it into the eight for the World Championships in 1999, but the team came away with the silver. Ben has had so many near-misses in his career and I think it says so much about the man that he didn't give up. He kept on training and kept on competing, no doubt because his vision of himself was as someone who did not quit. I honestly don't know if I could have carried on if my career had started the same way. Without the taste of victory to encourage and inspire me, I think I might have thrown in the towel.

For some reason, Ben just never got the winning habit, but his training paid off and he was selected to row in the eight for the Sydney Olympics. Watching him finally win a gold medal gave me greater pleasure than any other victory except my own. What's really interesting is that Ben then retired from rowing. He had finally got his gold and that was enough.

I wonder if I'd had a run of silvers and bronzes whether finally getting a gold would have made me quit too. When I look at people who start businesses when they are young, possibly earn good money from them or even sell them for a few million pounds, the evidence seems to suggest that they start a series of businesses and do it all over again. When someone who's a bit older starts a business, they seem more content to take the nest egg they've been offered and live a quieter life. I think there's definitely a component of enduring success that requires you to start, and succeed, young.

You get a taste for victory, you acquire the habit of winning, and the rest is just momentum.

Making momentum work for you

If you feel like momentum is going against you, you need to find a way to make it work for you. I reckon there are four stages to doing this: first you've got to *spot it*, or you've got to create it; then you've got to *build it*; then you *use it*. After that you also have to find a way to *keep it*. The good news is it's actually quite simple to do.

Every industry has momentum. For the past twenty years, if you've been in the technology sector, you will have seen companies and profits grow. If you've been in the manufacturing sector, the chances are you haven't. But even within shrinking sectors, there will have been momentum. If work that was once done in Britain is now outsourced to China, there will have been opportunities in freight and shipping, or in specialist project management where the overseas manufacturing process is overseen by people with knowledge of the Chinese economy. It takes too much energy to swim against the current, so it's vital that all your energy, vision, drive and dedication are focused in the right direction.

It's not just industries that have momentum: economies and countries do too. It's one of the reasons why Britain has been successful in winning bids to host major sporting events – the Olympics, the Commonwealth Games, the Rugby World Cup and hopefully the football World Cup will all be held on British soil in a 'golden decade' of sport between 2010 and 2020. We got good at bidding, we set up the right support for bid teams at government level and we funded them properly. Now those events will create momentum of their own for all sorts of companies, whether they build and manage sporting stadiums, arrange endorsements, do outside broadcasting or any number of other ancillary services.

Demographic changes can also create momentum. Britain has an ageing population, which means that a new business aimed at older consumers is more likely to do well than one in a country where the population is younger. Economic shifts can affect momentum too. The recession has seen many sectors reduce their workforce, but of course a recession actually creates jobs for some sectors, whether it's pawn brokers or the accountants who specialise in receivership. Those trainee accountants who chose the perhaps unfashionable path of specialising in receivership a few years ago are now looking very smart, and very employable. Whatever you do, wherever you do it, if you look around and make an assessment of where the momentum is going the chances are you will benefit.

> Truly great business leaders don't rely on using the momentum around them, they create their own.

Truly great business leaders don't rely on using the momentum around them, they create their own. One way to do this is through repetition, just like Roger Federer practising his drop shot or Jonny Wilkinson his drop kick. If you do something often enough you generally get better at it, whether it's selling to clients or using a piece of software. Mastering certain tasks leads to excellence, and when you are better at doing something better than anyone else, the tide has a habit of turning your way.

Another method is to start with simple, achievable tasks and build up your confidence. At every rowing regatta, teams almost always perform better in the final than the heats and that's partly because they've found their rhythm; the early, easy victories have given them confidence. It's true in most sports: easy victories in the early rounds of tournaments improve all aspects of players' performance. Going into a final on the back of a flawless run through the heats can do wonders for your confidence and your belief. You can use this method in business too: if you take on small jobs that you can complete to a very high standard, you don't just build your own confidence, you build the confidence that your clients have in you. Bigger jobs and bigger clients are more likely to follow than if you are too ambitious too soon when you're not up to the job.

Once you've found the momentum, you've got to know what to do with it. It's all very well anticipating that certain sectors are going to perform well, but if you want to benefit, you have to be willing to work in those sectors. Those people who consistently do well are prepared to change tack if circumstances require. Aligning yourself with momentum can take effort and planning, but if you aren't prepared to make the changes, then you won't stand to benefit.

The next step is the easy step – building momentum. The nature of momentum means that it very often builds itself. Good work leads to recommendations which lead to more work. Once the cycle is going in your favour, things can happen very rapidly. It's something I experienced when I came back from Sydney: all of a sudden the momentum was with me and I knew that if I didn't say yes to the offers that came my way in that very narrow window of time, they probably wouldn't come my way again. But because I started doing more public speaking at that point, I became better known for my public speaking, and so I was asked to do more of it. A decade on, and the work is still flowing.

Riding on a wave of momentum can be thrilling, but it can also be exhausting and possibly also a little bit frightening when things change so rapidly. Some people are tempted to take a breather and reflect on what's happening to them. They assume that they can take off from where they left things, but very often when they decide they want to continue their careers, the momentum has moved on. If you walk away from momentum, it is very hard to get it back.

Keeping hold of momentum is crucial to a long and successful career and the enduring successes in this book have all made sure that they've held on to the momentum they've generated. They do this by continually anticipating what's about to happen and putting in place strategies and teams that can benefit. If ever there was an example of a team that threw away momentum it was the England rugby union team. After winning the World Cup in 2003, the heroes of Sir Clive Woodward's side came home to find 750,000 people lining the streets of London to cheer their victory parade. For a few months, rugby had a prominence it had never previously enjoyed. This was the moment for rugby union to capitalise on its momentum. But what happened? The hierarchy decided that they wanted to go back to their old systems and they took away the infrastructure that had given Sir Clive Woodward and his team the platform to win the World Cup. Sir Clive resigned shortly afterwards, and captain Martin Johnson and several other senior team members announced their retirement from international rugby. And of course Jonny Wilkinson got injured.

Instead of lining up with experienced internationals, the new caps of 2004 had fewer people around them who could tell them what it was like to succeed at the highest level. Instead of inspiring a generation of schoolboys to want to become rugby players rather than football stars, England followed up victory with a series of embarrassing results. English rugby failed to turn its moment into momentum.

The rules of momentum are simple: find it, use it, build it and then keep it.

> **Case study**
>
> Name: David Lloyd
>
> Business: David Lloyd Leisure
>
> Years in business: 30

David Lloyd freely admits that he wasn't a great tennis player, but he is probably the most successful British sporting businessman. After a promising start – he won the junior titles at Wimbledon in singles and doubles in the same year – his senior career was eclipsed by the success of his younger brother John. Perhaps it was because he knew he wouldn't make his fortune in prize money, that he paid more attention as to how he would earn an income when he retired from the sport.

'A lot of players tend to retire, take a couple of years off and then try and pick up the threads, but by then of course their names – their value – have gone down, so I said to myself I'm going to do something while I'm still playing,' he says, displaying the common sense that helped him make a fortune. He didn't want to lose momentum. He knew he wanted to build indoor tennis clubs in the UK like those he had seen while he was touring. Wherever he went he inspected tennis facilities, making a note of what worked and what didn't. He started to draw up a business plan while he was still on the tour.

Business was not unfamiliar to him. The Lloyds were not a rich family, and to help pay for the costs of playing tennis, when the young David went round the world to play, his father – who was in the rag trade – sent him off with garments to sell. 'I was in South Africa as a seventeen-year-old, and instead of practising, I was selling crimplene dresses door-to-door. Crimplene makes you so hot it was ridiculous, but I literally wouldn't eat if I didn't sell them.'

David thought raising capital for his first tennis centre would be fairly straightforward, but after two years of being knocked back, he had to put his own money in. 'It was about £125k and it was all the money I had,' he recalls. 'Thankfully my wife at the time really believed in the idea. It was an enormous risk.'

Investing his own money gave him extra momentum. When you're that invested in the outcome, David believes you will work that much harder. 'These days I invest in other people's businesses, and one of the things I ask them is if they've put their own money in. It doesn't have to be a lot, but it has to be a big percentage of what they have. It just gives you the edge, the determination.'

His first club opened in Heston in 1980, and by the sounds of things, it was pretty chaotic. 'The clubs now have about ninety staff. We started with seventeen – we just didn't know how many we'd need – and it was literally twenty-four hours a day. I slept at the club. If it was busy at the bar, I'd serve drinks, if there was a leak I'd do a bit of plumbing. I was so paranoid because it was my name on the outside of the club that I felt I should do it without any help. I was so big headed that I felt I had to do it myself, but I soon learnt that you can't do it all yourself. And that's when I had to start picking people I trusted to delegate to.

'Getting the right people to manage the clubs was vital. We had to have people who could *do* whatever was required – balance the books or sit on reception – and be smart enough to *know* what was required. My people weren't necessarily university graduates, they were just people with huge amounts of common sense.'

Some of those people are still with him today. One of the reasons David Lloyd staff are so loyal is because of the company's share option scheme. 'Most share option schemes favour the board members: we were the opposite. The people at the bottom of the company got four times the allocation, in proportion to their salary, as the people at the top. The guy on £10k could do really well working for us and he worked his arse off.' When David sold the business to Whitbread, reportedly for £200m in 1985, a few of his team did indeed become millionaires.

As well as being properly incentivised, David also made sure they were properly managed. 'Everyone reported to me directly, and they still do,' he says. 'When you have a pyramidal management structure, I found that you were creating layers of bureaucracy that meant people could pass the buck. Responsibility for things was passed down the chain. When I sold the business to Whitbread, they brought in different management structures and the business suffered.' The business has since been bought back from Whitbread and David's son Scott is the CEO.

The huge success of the Heston club meant David Lloyd tennis centres were rolled out rapidly. 'At one point we opened four clubs in one week. The City said it couldn't be done. Well, we did it and they were all full.' Once they were geared up for expansion, momentum took over and by 1985 there were eighteen David Lloyd Leisure Centres. With each new club, the formula was improved. 'I started doing what we call "zero budgeting" which means you start each year with a new sheet of paper and do your sums all over again, starting from zero.' It's very easy, as companies grow, to not notice how inefficient your business is because you focus on the fact that revenues are increasing and forget to see just how fast your costs are also increasing. 'You look at that piece of paper and go, "Christ, I've got seven receptionists. I only need five." It's so easy for a profitable business to carry costs it doesn't need to.'

David also questioned why they were outsourcing cleaning, or crèche facilities. 'I realised we were paying a firm of architects £400k to design a club. It was cheaper to employ my own architect. We brought everything in-house and we got better and smarter with each club.' These efficiencies meant more profits, which meant more clubs.

David stayed on as Managing Director for a year after he sold the business to Whitbread, and has since been involved in a number of other businesses, including the Next Generation chain of health clubs. The business that gets him most excited these days is his overseas property company that builds luxury villas and apartments for international investors. 'I realised that after building so many health clubs, I had learnt a lot about planning, property and construction,' he says.

His business career has acquired the kind of momentum that you get when you combine expertise with experience: look at Roger Federer – he has become almost unstoppable. David might not have had Roger's success on the court, but off the court, his momentum shows no sign of slowing down.

11

THE POWER OF COMMUNICATION

Early on in my career, one of the very few sources of income I had was from the SportsAid Foundation. It wasn't a lot of money – about £5,000 a year – but it was by far and away my single biggest source of funding. The SportsAid money kept me in rowing. Although we were awarded the grants as individuals, the applications were channelled through British Rowing. I have a very clear memory of one of the coaches coming into the gym at the end of a training session with a sheaf of cheques in his hand.

'*I've* got *your* cheque here, Steve. Here you go.'

It's a really old trick I was familiar with from working

on building sites as a teenager. Once a week the foreman would come round with little brown envelopes to give us our wages in person. It was a very unsubtle way of saying: 'I'm in charge and you're not.' That coach wanted me to feel that he was the one giving me the money and not the SportsAid Foundation.

I can't imagine Bill Gates or Martin Sorrell or Peter Jones adopting this kind of approach. Great leaders know about the importance of communication because they know that it's not just *what* you say that counts, but also *how* you say it. Things have changed since the days of the SportsAid grants.

Good communication is not about being a good or clear speaker; it is pretty much to do with saying the right thing at the right time in the right way. In my sport, when you're in the middle of a race and your muscles are in agony and it feels as though your lungs are on fire, you're not about to have a conversation about how you all think the race is going. Sometimes making yourself heard over the noise of the boat and the water takes more effort than you've got left. Some days all I could say was 'now'; some days the other guys in the boat had to interpret my grunts. It was not the right time to talk tactics.

But we didn't need to. We had spent years preparing for those races and we had discussed our race plans for hours on end. We all knew what 'now' meant, and assuming that we were all fit and well, we all knew exactly how the others were feeling. I knew who hurt most in the opening strokes, and who felt it worst in the final metres. Our communication had been done during those long days of training.

One of the key elements of our communication was the agreement that I would be the one calling the race. If I decided it was time to up our stroke rate, we couldn't have a situation where the others thought we shouldn't. Matthew told me early on in our career together that I'd called a race and he hadn't agreed with my tactics. The potential problem in that situation is that if you don't believe in the tactics, you're not going to believe it's going to get the result so you're not going to work as hard. But Matthew had decided at some point during our training that whatever I called, he was going to give 100 per cent. He reasoned that we could discuss his concerns after the race and incorporate them into the next race. He knew that mid-race was not the time to discuss things, so whatever I called, his response was to follow my lead.

I really admired Matt for that. It isn't easy to follow an instruction you don't believe in, but good teams have to pull in the same direction and sometimes that means suppressing individual ideas for the benefit of the team. I have been in the same situation myself rowing in coxed crews. Every so often a cox would make a call that seemed nonsensical to me, but it wasn't my job to argue, it was my job to respond to his commands.

One of the best communicators I've come across in my research for this book is Dame Anita Roddick, the founder of The Body Shop. Her business was completely different from other shops selling cosmetics and beauty products. When she opened her first shop in 1976, she didn't just have to tell customers about the fact The Body Shop existed, she had to communicate why it was different (there are so many 'green' cosmetic products now it's hard to remember just how different The Body Shop was back then). Other companies spent a fortune on branding and packaging, but all her products were lined up on the shelves in identikit bottles. While other cosmetic firms spent a fortune on testing their products on animals, Roddick not only needed to convey that she didn't test her products, she needed to explain why that was important because most of her customers hadn't thought about the cruelty aspect of cosmetics. Later, as her business grew, she became one of the early pioneers of the fair trade movement, paying indigenous communities a premium for their wares.

Roddick wasn't just selling cosmetics, she was selling a philosophy. Whether she knew it or not, she was giving people a reason to choose her products over someone else's. That, at the most fundamental level, is the basis of a good sales technique: giving someone the information they need to choose to buy from you.

Almost everyone featured in this book has had to communicate a complex message to large groups of people, whether that's their staff or their customers. When Microsoft introduces a new piece of software, it doesn't just have to announce the launch, it has to explain what the software does and why potential customers will benefit from using its product over a rival's. When Terry Leahy wants to introduce a new line of products into Tesco, he needs to explain his decision to his shareholders, his staff and his customers. If you can't communicate, you're not going to be very successful.

Communicating effectively

When I talked about vision in the first chapter, I said that the power of someone's vision can only be realised if they are able to communicate their vision. Equally, if you are working in an organisation that's badly managed, there's no point in moaning to your co-workers about it – you have to take it up with your boss if you want something to change. What matters about communication is that it is *effective*. There are four simple steps to effective communication: *know what you want to say, know who to say it to, know how to say it* and *know when to say it.*

I used to do a bit of garden landscaping when I was younger and I occasionally had customers who wanted me to lay a patio or lawn, and they would say things like 'I'd like a patio here' and not realise that I'd also need to know how big they wanted the patio to be, what materials they wanted it made out of, when they wanted it done by or what their budget was. Some would look out of their windows and see me at work and come out and tell me I was doing it wrong! Only when I had started work could they see that the patio was in the wrong place or was the wrong size or any number of other observations. I stood there thinking: *why on earth couldn't you have told me this earlier?* If I had been more experienced, I might have been able to ask the right questions to get the right information needed, but what usually happened was the clients who could tell me what they wanted got what they wanted, whereas those that couldn't had to live with whatever I thought they'd said they'd wanted. Those that gave me clear instructions before I started work usually had a happier landscape gardener who did better work!

Whether you're asking someone to lay a lawn, design a new product or cut costs in their department, you need to be clear about what you want. You need to work out what information people need to do their work to the standard and specifications you want. What's their deadline, what's the criteria for success, what are the consequences of not completing the work? Tell them why it's important. Let them know if other people are relying on them to meet their deadline.

You also need to make sure you are giving the information to the right person, in the right situation. If you have a problem with an advertising campaign, it's better to take that up with the advertising manager in a private meeting rather than a board meeting in front of the rest of the team. The manner in which messages are delivered can often have as much impact as the message. Feedback, for instance, is always more readily received than criticism.

> There is one single factor in the communication style of truly successful people: they don't just talk, they listen.

Having spent time in the past decade observing people who run large corporations and international charities, I have noticed that there is one single factor in the communication style of truly successful people: they don't just talk, they listen. They ask for input from their staff and feedback from their customers. Communication in an organisation has to be two-way. When people feel listened to, they also tend to feel loyal.

Richard Branson is particularly good at listening. He has an unusual policy of inviting Virgin employees – from every Virgin business, and from every level of the business – to come up with new ideas for the company. If he likes their idea, he'll back it, which is why Virgin has moved into areas like wines, bridal boutiques and cosmetics. Some of these ventures have been a lot more successful than others, but I suspect the incalculable benefit to Branson is a motivated staff who are loyal both to Virgin and to him.

The Virgin vibe is transmitted throughout the Virgin organisation. Branson has found ways for his staff to feel that their employer cares about their welfare, and about how much fun they are having. Branson wants Virgin to be seen as a 'fun' brand: what better way to communicate that to his customers than for every single member of his team to greet their customers with a genuine smile? If Virgin is fun to work for, the logic goes that it must also be fun to buy from.

Virgin manages to put a smile on its workforce – or 'tribe' as they are called – by having a generous in-house reward scheme that offers discounts on Virgin flights and other purchases. Joining the Branson tribe is like joining a private club with its own website, membership card and benefits (including discounted shopping with retail partners). Branson sees Virgin as a different kind of company, and fostering his tribe is a unique way of communicating that.

If you've ever bought anything from Virgin, you'll probably have noticed that their communication with their customers is very informal. Their letters start with 'Hello' rather than 'Dear Sir or Madam'. They say 'thanks' instead of 'thank you' and they don't ask you to call 'customer services' if you've got a problem, they ask you to call the 'team'. Virgin doesn't do anything that lots of other companies don't also do (whether it's trains, planes, publishing or broadband, they're not the only operator in those markets), but they do everything that bit differently. This is because they know who they're talking to. They are trying to reach a youth market, and their message is tailored to that market. They know what they want to say, they know who they want to say it to and they know how to say it.

I now try hard to encourage the organisations I'm involved with to improve their communications. My success at the Olympics has meant that when I talk, people within sporting organisations will listen to me for a few minutes longer than they would to someone who walked in off the street, and I try and use those minutes to make them see how very small changes to the methods and channels of communication inside these organisations can make big differences to the people who work for them.

I hope that by showing chief executives and senior staff in these sporting bodies the benefits of thinking about *what* they're saying and *how* it's being received will mean that when today's athletes receive their funding, it will be handled with a lot more sensitivity than when I used to get my cheques.

> **Case study**
> Name: Sir Martin Sorrell
> Business: WPP advertising
> Years in business: 25

'Being in advertising is rather like sport in that you're only as good as your last performance.' Sir Martin Sorrell, CEO of the world's largest advertising and media agency WPP knows what he's talking about. The fickle nature of his industry makes his success all the more remarkable.

For the CEO of a FTSE 100 company, Sorrell's background is both pretty conventional *and* unusual. He's a Cambridge graduate who also attended the prestigious Harvard Business School, which might make you think his success is a simple consequence of his education. But other facts about his career make you realise he is far from your average corporate titan. For starters, he didn't start WPP until he was forty (he says he went through a 'male menopause') and he has now been at the helm for twenty-five years, which is a practically unique achievement in an era when the average CEO tenure is under five years. What really makes him stand out from other business leaders, however, is that he founded the business he still runs. As he says himself: 'People who found businesses are not usually good at running businesses, and people who run businesses are not usually good at founding them.'

After graduating from Harvard, Sorrell worked for a number of companies – including the management company IMG where he was briefly Jackie Stewart's manager – and eventually became the finance director at Saatchi & Saatchi, which was then thought of as the world's most creative advertising agency. Sorrell's idea was to apply his business training to a creative company and run it more efficiently than his rivals. To that end, he – along with his associate Preston Rabl – raised £1m in loans to buy a business called Wire & Plastic Products, a publicly listed manufacturer of wire baskets for supermarkets. His intention was to use WPP as a vehicle to buy up existing advertising agencies, and within two years he had made ten acquisitions, one of which was one of the world's best-known ad agencies in J Walter Thompson (JWT). The purchase of one of the industry's biggest names by one of its newest entrants created quite a stir and sealed Sorrell's reputation as a formidable deal maker.

In the past twenty years, WPP has continued to make acquisitions and now agencies that were previously rivals are all under the same roof. Sir Martin has made these mergers and takeovers work because he understands – as you would expect from someone in the ad game – the importance of communication.

'I think if your growth hasn't come through acquisition, then communication within the business is probably easier,' he says. 'Acquisitions make it more difficult, but more important.' It's further complicated by the fact that two or more of WPP's subsidiaries may be competing against each other for the same contract. Some brands within WPP are what we call "frenemies", but people cooperate whenever there are opportunities or challenges, and over the past ten years that degree of cooperation has increased.'

That is down to the company's impressive internal communications structures. As well as introducing in-house publications and annual awards that reward excellence, Sorrell has structured the company so that knowledge and talent is shared. 'When I started WPP there were two of us; now there are 140,000 employees. It would be great if everyone knew the other 139,999, but clearly that's not going to happen. However, it is important that they know what other people are doing. One of the great things about a company like ours that started small is that you really appreciate the contribution of every individual who joins the team. When we acquire a business that is perhaps 150 years old, they might have a different attitude because they think they've seen it all before. When you mix cultures, it's critically important that you find ways of getting people to work together.'

One of the ways WPP ensures its different companies learn about each other is through its staffing structures. 'We get people who work in the different verticals, the different companies, to act on a horizontal basis across the company. We identify departments that would benefit from working together and we make sure their information, their knowledge is shared.'

It's also hard for an umbrella organisation like WPP to both stand with its subsidiaries and at the same time be distinct from them. Should employees feel that they are working for JWT, or WPP? Good communication means they can feel they are working for both without a sense of conflict.

Some companies might think that simply producing an in-house magazine or an intranet is enough to get messages to staff and to help employees develop a sense of corporate identity, but Sir Martin understands that communication doesn't start and end with the written word. You also communicate through your values. 'We invest in our staff, we don't just pay them. We invest in incentivising, motivating and keeping people, which is difficult in a business like ours, but we want people to want to work here. We invested $1bn in property making our buildings green and tackling climate change because we think that makes us more efficient. We invest in systems and procedures that make our people more effective.' When staff see their bosses spending money on things like that, I think it's fairly natural that they develop an idea about their parent company's corporate identity. By doing this, Sorrell is effectively telling his staff 'I care about you', which is just about the most powerful sentiment a boss can communicate to his team.

WPP is a truly global business with people working on every continent in several languages. 'I think you increasingly have to be comfortable with things being a bit messy. If you look at the management structures that were advocated at the beginning of the twentieth century, they look incredibly staid and outmoded. Those military organisations that rank employees in a pyramid structure aren't responding to how people really work.'

These days, an employee can work out the boss's email address and get in touch directly. Blogs and intranets mean people from all over an organisation are in touch with each other, and the idea that there are 'proper' channels of communication looks increasingly old-fashioned. Improved communication makes it easier for the best ideas to surface, and modern CEOs need to be able to deal with that. 'Messy works. Confusion works. Chaos works. The only way you are going to get people working together is if you get rid of your hierarchies and replace them with networks; that's the best way to get people learning from one another.'

12

THE IMPORTANCE OF LEADERSHIP

I was the fourth person to get involved with the London 2012 bid. Shortly after the Sydney Olympics, I was approached by the British Olympic Association to test the waters about putting a bid together. At the time the only other people involved were the chief executive of the BOA, Simon Clegg, the chairman Sir Craig Reedie and also an IOC member and a hockey player called David Lucas who had been asked to do some research for them in Sydney. They hoped that by bringing me on board, I could open a few doors and set up meetings. One of the first people I spoke to was the then Mayor of London, Ken Livingstone.

I had expected the mayor's reaction to be 'too expensive, too distracting', but to his credit Ken immediately saw the benefits of bringing the Olympics to London and got right behind the bid. From that moment on, we started approaching the people whose support we would need and the team of four quickly became a team of ten, then twenty, then thirty . . . Once we had decided on a site for the Olympic village, officials from the four neighbouring local authorities needed to be involved, and each official had several assistants. Put them together with representatives from the mayor's office, the Prime Minister's office, the Department for Culture, Media and Sport, and it's easy to see how the bid team got so big. I sat in on one meeting and thought to myself: this is never going to work, no one's in charge. What we needed was leadership.

I needn't have worried. When Barbara Cassani walked into her first meeting as the newly appointed chair of the bid team, it was clear she knew what she was doing. I still didn't know much about Barbara except that she had been responsible for setting up Go Airlines, BA's low-cost subsidiary, and that she was American. There had been quite a few mutterings that an American should not be leading the British bid, but at that first meeting those mutterings stopped. Barbara did an amazing job of making all the different stakeholders in the bid feel listened to and valued, and then she did something really tough: she made decisions that she knew not everyone would agree with. There was no way that a group of thirty people with different priorities would reach a consensus, and Barbara knew this. She knew it would be down to her to make choices, hire the right people and get the bid submitted in time.

In truth I think the fact that we had left making a bid relatively late worked to her advantage. Quick decisions were the only option if we were to make the International Olympic Committee's deadline for submission, and Barbara was able to use this as a reason to consult a little less and implement a little more. When she stepped down as chair of the bid, Seb Coe was appointed and he did a fantastic job of selling the bid to put us in the running.

Over the years I have worked with some very good leaders, as well as a few I've had issues with, and Barbara stands out as someone who had the best combination of the organisational capabilities, vision and personal skills that make for great leadership. I've already mentioned a rowing coach who made a point of handing out 'his' grant cheques, and there were others who ran the sport without consulting athletes or coaches or who didn't have the personal skills to inspire the competitors.

My success in rowing in effect made me a figurehead

for the sport, and at times that has brought me into conflict with the powers that be in British Rowing. If the press wanted an opinion on rowing, they would want a quote from me, not the chief executive. I can see that this caused problems for the organisation, but it was a situation that could have been handled much better. We all know when we are working for a good leader, and we all know how much harder it is to do your best work when your leader undermines or undervalues you. Good leadership can transform an organisation, and good leaders are the ones whose careers endure. Look at Sir Alex Ferguson: it's no coincidence that he is both the longest-serving manager in the Premier League *and* its most successful.

So what are the qualities of good leadership? To start with I would have to say that basic management skills are a must. To inspire confidence in your team you at least have to be competent. Salaries need to be paid, raw materials need to be ordered in sufficient quantities by the required date and staff need to work in a safe environment. Without those basics, any team is going to be demoralised and not incentivised to do their best work. Very often leaders of large organisations will delegate these responsibilities to a general manager – in fact, they almost certainly should as good leadership is not about micro-managing – but good leaders are never so far out of touch with their workforce that they don't know that the basics are being covered.

I think it goes without saying that there are two other qualities that are universally found in all good leaders: they are good at delegation *and* they are good at building a team to delegate to. They are always on the lookout for talented individuals that will fit into their team, and they are also good at finding roles for the right people. Once you have people on your team that you trust, delegating to them becomes so much easier. And once tasks are delegated, the leader can focus on offering the strategic vision that companies need to grow and move forward.

Good leaders have to be figureheads for their organisations, which means they have to inspire their workers as well as their customers. Being a figurehead can be a bit of a balancing act: you need to reveal enough of yourself so that people can relate to you and feel loyal to you; yet you also need to keep enough of a distance so that when it's time to be tough, you are able to deliver difficult news. Over the years I have seen many leaders excel at inspiring their teams, but they have made the mistake of becoming too friendly with their staff and customers. A big part of leadership is the ability to say 'no', and if you are too close to people to be able to say it, then you start to make the wrong decisions and success begins to waver.

> *A great deal of good leadership is about balance.*

In fact a great deal of good leadership is about balance. Whether it's weighing up letting your staff enjoy themselves with the need to get the work done, or balancing the demands of shareholders against the demands of customers, leaders often walk a very fine line. They need to be in touch with the shop floor, and often that means being seen on the shop floor and spending time with the workforce, but they simultaneously need to keep enough distance to make decisions and develop strategy. It's no wonder then, that really good leaders are rare; and it's also no wonder that when we find ourselves working for a good leader, we also find ourselves working that bit harder.

Leadership usually comes with a side serving of pressure and the ability to operate effectively under the weight of that pressure is crucial. Towards the end of my rowing career, when I was seen by many commentators as the 'leader' of the crews I rowed in, I felt the pressure very keenly. I knew that people were looking to me to bring home a medal, and I knew that how I handled the pressure would affect how the other guys in the crew would handle it. I think that is the one area where I was genuinely able to set an example, but in every other regard the label of 'leader' was wrong. We were all equal, all equal contributors. Nevertheless, I understand how difficult it is to perform when everyone is looking to you to perform. No one wants to see their boss unsure: people take their cues from their boss and if their boss can't project an image of confidence, then it will affect the entire organisation. Being a leader in any organisation is a little bit like being famous: any tiny slip-ups will be exposed and talked about by the in-house gossips rather than the ones who write for newspapers.

I once heard a great quote: 'Dictators talk, leaders listen.' Like all good lines, it's only partially true because great leaders have to do a great deal of talking, but the listening part is definitely true. Good leaders listen to their customers, their staff, industry opinion and their rivals. They soak up information that enables them to make the right decision for their company. You can only succeed in the long term if your business, your service or your product somehow makes people happier. You might give them lower prices or better service or better quality, but somehow your activities have to make their lives better. You can only know if you are doing this if you listen to what people tell you. I sit on boards for several charities, and I can tell you that it's not always the people who do the most talking at some of those meetings who contribute the most.

Above all, the quality a leader has to have to successfully steer an organisation is authority. People must believe what the leader says to such a degree that they will go along with whatever he or she has said. Whether a leader is liked by their staff, or feared by them, authority is the attribute that ensures the work gets done. The single most important way a leader can do this, in my experience, is by making the right decisions. Anyone who is dithering is not leading, and an organisation that is not being led is not moving towards enduring success.

Decision making is both an art and a science. There are some people who diligently make lists of the pros and cons of their various options and there are some people who trust their hunches so much that they make decisions in the blink of an eye. What I have learnt over the years is that it doesn't really matter how you make a decision, it simply matters that you make it. If you don't get into the habit of making decisions, you can find yourself drowning in indecision, and nothing slows

188

progress down like indecision. I truly believe that decision making is a habit, because the more often you are called on to make a decision, the more accustomed you become to the emotions and responsibilities that come with decision making.

Clear and swift decision making by the boss can save the entire organisation from wasting effort and time on the wrong course of action. Indecision doesn't just have a financial cost, it has an emotional cost too, because everyone can sense when they are working for a dynamic organisation, just as they can sense when that organisation loses its way. It's probably why a lot of successful people offer an unusual piece of advice about decision making: very often a bad decision is better than no decision. The logic behind this is that bad decisions give you a chance to learn something about yourself and your business that might be useful in the future. Indecision ultimately means your business is going nowhere – a decision, even a bad one, can keep your momentum going.

> **Case study**
> Name: Sir Alex Ferguson
> Organisation: Manchester United manager
> Years in charge: 24

Sir Alex has been in charge at Manchester United since 1986 and in those twenty-four years he has won more trophies than anyone else in European football. When United won the treble in 1999 – the FA Cup, the Premier League and the Champions League – most commentators assumed that the newly knighted Sir Alex would retire on a high. Eleven years on and he's still there, and still winning.

His achievements are usually listed in the form of trophies: the FA Cup (five times), the League Cup (four times), the Premier League title (an incredible eleven times), the Champions League (twice), not to mention UEFA titles, Charity Shields and the FIFA Club World Cup. However, I think his greatest achievement is successfully managing twenty or thirty young millionaires who regularly get their egos stroked by thousands of people cheering their name. How do you discipline a twenty-year-old millionaire who knows ten other clubs would love to have him? For that reason, I think Alex Ferguson is probably the best leader of men of his generation. I'm not alone in thinking that. Tony Fitzpatrick, who captained St Mirren under Ferguson, once said that Fergie had 'the gift of leadership'. Martin O'Neill, the Aston Villa manager, called him 'the greatest manager in the game'.

Manchester United players must get used to getting things their own way. They are rich enough to buy whatever they want, and they probably have staff that can get them anything they fancy, whether it's a yacht for the weekend or a diamond-encrusted iPhone. But there's one place where their fame and their millions count for nothing – at Manchester United's training ground. All that matters there is how hard they work and the results they produce.

It's been reported that Ferguson regularly works eighteen-hour days. He will keep his players at the training ground long after the floodlights have been switched on and not let them go until he is satisfied with their performance. Other managers might tell them to 'go away and practise', but Ferguson stays with them. When you see a man who is old enough to be your grandfather putting in the hours, it's no wonder so many of United's young players don't shirk in training.

At other clubs, you get the sense that the manager isn't always the one in charge. Sometimes it's the chairman who pulls the strings, and sometimes individual players seem to have more power than the manager. Other teams would never dream of leaving players like Wayne Rooney and Cristiano Ronaldo on the bench, but Ferguson regularly leaves his star players out of his starting line-up. He selects the right team for the match.

Ferguson has a reputation for being tough, but bullies don't inspire respect. He may have a tough exterior, but he also must have insight and intuition: how else could he have persuaded Wayne Rooney and Cristiano Ronaldo to play together after Ronaldo had successfully got Wayne Rooney sent off when England played Portugal in the 2006 World Cup quarter-final? Sure, Ferguson could have knocked heads together and told them to get on with it, but the 2006/7 season saw the two young players produce some of their best football, often setting each other up to score. Ferguson has an amazing ability to turn enemies into teammates.

I imagine one of the reasons why top players accept Sir Alex's decisions is because he is both loyal and protective towards his players. He never bad-mouths his players to the press, and any dissatisfaction he feels about their performance is always expressed in private. Whether it was Roy Keane storming out of the Ireland team during the World Cup, or David Beckham getting red carded for England, Ferguson always backed his players to the hilt.

Even when it seemed clear that Ferguson had grown weary of the media circus that surrounded David Beckham in his final seasons at the club, Ferguson never gave the press the quote they wanted about the reported rift between the two. In a sport where backbiting and leaks to the press are the norm, it's no wonder that players respond to Ferguson's loyalty.

Of course, it's not just the players who are loyal to Ferguson: the fans are too. You would expect a manager that keeps bringing home the silverware to remain popular, but what's interesting is how Ferguson's track record becomes self-perpetuating: he wins, so the fans love him and the players respect him; the loyalty he inspires means people work harder, and the extra effort means United keep winning.

Ferguson's achievements give him authority. Much has been made of the success of Manchester United's youth programme that has created players like Beckham, Ryan Giggs, Paul Scholes, Wes Brown and the Neville brothers, and it's easy to imagine just how deferential young players would be to a manager with Ferguson's reputation. But that still doesn't explain how he gets the best out of so many players over such a long period of time. Peter Schmeichel, who kept goal in United's all-conquering 1998/9 season, reveals that the man who is famous for speaking in as few words as possible is actually a very skilled communicator. 'You have to earn his respect, but it's clear what he wants,' he said. That clarity is, I think, the key to getting a team to work together. Schmeichel continued: 'He doesn't care how you live your life as long as you give him consistent levels of effort and performance. Do that, and he trusts you. Fergie could be so aggressive, yet once he'd got a problem out into the open, it was gone. There are thousands of better coaches. Coaching isn't Fergie's strength. But management? The handling of men? There's nobody better.'

13

INTEGRITY

One of the businesses I've been involved with since retiring from sport is the FiveG clothing brand. As I described earlier, I was approached by the Ruia Group to put my name to a range of leisurewear, and after a few initial problems – like advertising the stock before we'd checked the quality of the merchandise – we secured distribution through independent retailers and an online service. For a couple of years, things ticked along nicely enough, but I couldn't help noticing that it wasn't making me very much money.

I had regular meetings with the team and kept on expecting them to quietly pull the plug. After all, if something's not making money, you'd be better off spending your time on something that delivers a profit.

I had even got to the stage where I thought that I should be the one to call time on the operation.

However, just before I got to that stage, I had a review meeting with Alok Ruia, the younger brother of the Ruia family who had just taken over the range. He suggested that FiveG might benefit from making clothing using fair trade cotton. I didn't know enough about fair trade to say whether it would work, but finding out more about fair trade seemed to fit in well with some of the charity work I was doing. Alok's idea turned out to be a winner: we clinched a deal with Debenhams to become the fair trade arm of their in-house brand Maine of New England.

One of the happy side effects of having a public profile is that you get invited to do things that wouldn't happen if you weren't well known. When we got in touch with the Fairtrade Foundation, which accredits fair trade imports, they asked if I would be interested in going out to Mali to meet fair trade cotton producers. I jumped at the chance.

The fair trade system guarantees payments for producers in developing countries in advance. It also includes a small premium for community projects. Knowing that they will receive a fixed price for their goods gives the farmers stability they otherwise wouldn't have. It gives them some certainty in what, for many, is still a very precarious existence. Debenhams and I decided that we would absorb the fair trade premium ourselves and offer our fair trade clothing to shoppers at the same price as non-fair trade clothes.

In Mali, I was taken to two villages, one where the farmers are part of the fair trade scheme, and one where they are not. The difference between the two villages was startling. The thing that really struck me about the fair trade village was the thing they had spent their extra income on was not a well, a school or a medical centre – it was a large storage barn. But as I talked to the villagers, I started to understand why. The cotton harvest takes two to three weeks, and without storage, some of the cotton gets ruined before it can be processed. The barn is also used to store edible crops, because before the barn was built, the village had no option but to sell its harvest while it was fresh to people in towns and cities with storage facilities. For the rest of the year, they were buying these crops back in smaller quantities at higher prices from the people with their own barns. I would never have thought that the priority for any community would be storage, but that one simple barn enabled an entire village to be more prosperous, and with prosperity came improvements in education and healthcare.

The reason I'm sharing this story here is because

once FiveG started using fair trade cotton – and, perhaps more importantly, once I understood the importance of using fair trade cotton – something interesting happened to FiveG. Our sales figures started improving, and shortly after that, so did our profits. And this was even though we were absorbing the fair trade premium. So what happened? Well, I think integrity happened.

> When you do something with integrity, people respond.

Once everyone involved in FiveG became aware of just what could be achieved by using fair trade cotton, something very subtle shifted in our thinking. I think we became that little bit more proud of what we were doing, possibly a little more committed, and when we talked to potential customers, I'm sure we did it with more conviction. It must have helped that there were already customers out there who were actively seeking a fair trade alternative, but I also think there were people who chose FiveG clothes because they sensed that FiveG had become a brand with values. They simply responded to our greater effort and greater commitment. When you do something with integrity, people respond.

Organisations that stand for something other than profit are more likely to inspire loyalty in both staff and customers and are therefore more likely to endure.

The people profiled in this book reveal their integrity in different ways. David Lloyd, for example, inspires his team with a share option scheme. His employees aren't just working for him, they are working for themselves and they will enjoy a share of the company's success. When David sold his leisure centre business to Whitbread in 1995, he wasn't the only one to receive a sizeable cheque: several of his employees became millionaires too. I can't be sure, but I imagine that if David's workforce had thought they were working for a money-grabbing tyrant, they might not have worked quite so hard, and David Lloyd Leisure might not have been such a successful business. Caring about your staff and caring that your customers are satisfied really is at the heart of corporate integrity.

Win/win

As I've spoken to people for this book, one phrase has kept coming up: win/win. Successful people don't look for deals where they benefit, they look for deals where everyone benefits. You could look at a business and see it as a series of deals, and if you are constantly trying to win over partners to do your next deal with, you will expend an awful lot of energy. If, on the other hand, you can go back to the person you did your last deal with, you will probably have a much easier time. Repeat business requires having a relationship with your customers and your suppliers, and you can only build those relationships if everyone benefits from the deals. Win/win. Businesses and individuals that seek to maximise profits at the expense of personal relationships with customers and staff find long-term success much harder to come by.

You can tell a lot about a person's integrity by looking at how they spend their money. Microsoft founder Bill Gates frequently finds himself at the top of the global Rich List with a personal fortune of somewhere between $30bn and $40bn. Some billionaires spend their money on yachts and helicopters; Gates chose to set up his own charitable foundation. He has pledged over $10bn to research, develop and distribute vaccines that could prevent hundreds of thousands of deaths in the developing world each year.

The man who has vied with Gates for the title of the world's richest person over the past decade is the American investor Warren Buffett (although as of 2010, they have both lost that crown to the Mexican telecoms

owner Carlos Slim). Unlike Gates, who set up a foundation that bears his name, Buffett realised that he did
not have to set up his own foundation precisely because
Gates had already done it. Warren Buffett pledged
$31bn to the Bill and Melinda Gates Foundation
because he realised that Gates was the man who had the
expertise to deploy his cash wisely. For anyone who
thinks extraordinary wealth and integrity are incom-
patible, Warren Buffett proves them very wrong.

Gates employs tens of thousands of people, whereas
Buffett famously runs his investment company with
just a handful of staff, but I'd be willing to bet that both
of their teams prefer to work for the kind of billionaire
who uses his wealth to save lives than one who is constantly photographed on his super-yacht. The benefit of
Gates and Buffett's generosity isn't just felt by those
who receive their donations.

It's interesting to me how readily wealthy people are
willing to become involved in charitable foundations. I
think this is because they are forced to consider what
the point of money is in a way the rest of us aren't
because we're so busy finding enough money to pay our
rent and bills. That might sound strange, but once the
really rich have taken care of their family and friends,
once they've bought themselves the classic sports car
they've always coveted, when they've got enough

money to buy whatever they want, there's certainly no incentive for them to carry on working purely for the money. For them, money only means something if they can do something meaningful with it. When each new deal represents a smaller and smaller percentage of your overall wealth, it is less likely to motivate you. Knowing that a deal will benefit their philanthropic endeavours, or will foster loyalty among staff or customers, is far more likely to keep them interested. Integrity keeps them going.

Certainly, integrity is at the core of Comic Relief's continued ability to raise millions of pounds, and it's one of the many reasons why I am committed to my role on the board of Comic Relief. When I am raising funds for Comic Relief, it is great to be able to say to donors that every single penny raised goes to good causes. We've all heard stories over the years about money that's been raised by charities which has somehow disappeared in overheads and poor management. The public know that doesn't happen with Sport Relief and Comic Relief and they are seen as organisations with integrity because of it. We know that people have worked hard to earn the money they donate, and it would be disrespectful to squander it.

Respect is at the core of integrity. People who have achieved enduring success retain a respect for the qualities that helped them achieve their success in the first place – hard work, talent, dedication, perseverance – and they do not ask the people around them to waste their time and effort on projects and endeavours that do not benefit both parties. People like Sir Jackie Stewart have an amazing ability to phone up heads of state or industry leaders and get them to agree to meetings. They are able to do this because they have utmost respect for their partners' time and they would not take proposals to them that were not worth their while. Truly successful people don't believe that their success makes them better than anyone else: they know that as soon as they start to value their own abilities above those of the people around them, they start to lose their integrity.

I can't stress how much I believe integrity is at the heart of long-term success. I just don't believe it's possible to achieve enduring success on your own, and if you require people to help you succeed, you have to take care of the people who help you. Whether those people are your customers, your employees, your family or business partners, if you treat people badly you will soon find yourself alone. If money was the only thing the people in this book cared about, I think they would have been far less successful.

> **Case study**
> Name: Sir Jackie Stewart
> Business: Stewart Grand Prix, Rolex, Moët &
> Chandon
> Years in business: 37

Before Jackie Stewart became a three-time world champion racing driver, he had been a world-class clay pigeon shooter who competed for Britain and twice won the Coupe de Nations. Since he retired from racing in 1973, Sir Jackie has launched a succession of companies and been an ambassador for some of the world's biggest brands. Within a few minutes of meeting him you realise that it didn't matter what walk of life he chose, he would always have been successful. And after a couple of hours in his company you understand why: integrity.

Whatever he does, Sir Jackie makes sure he does it to the very best of his ability. As a teenager he worked at his father's garage washing cars and filling tanks, and he earned more in tips than he did in wages because he did such a good job. 'I was busy trying to please people and get them to like me.' He thinks this is because he had been bullied and beaten up at school for being 'thick' – he's actually dyslexic – and was keen to find rewards from work that he never got from school. It was one of the garage's customers who first asked him if he wanted to race as a way of thanking him for taking such good care of his car. 'If there was a world championship for cleaning windows or sweeping floors, I would have won it,' he says. 'My attention to detail is my biggest asset. In my businesses, I am the president of the menial task division. The other day I was in the Scottish parliament building and I picked up some litter. "Don't worry about that," the guy I was with said. But I knew it shouldn't be there so I picked it up and put it in the bin.' If something's wrong, he wants to put it right.

Sir Jackie's dyslexia gave him the drive to be successful later in life. 'Learning disabilities didn't exist in those days. I was in a class of fifty-four and it was easier to ignore me than to teach me. I think when I left school this gave me a real hunger to be good at something. I still can't read or write well. I don't know the alphabet and I don't know the words to the Lord's Prayer or the national anthem. I don't mind saying that now, but as a kid it was humiliating, and that gives you the drive to prove yourself.'

It was clay pigeon shooting that first gave him the opportunity to shine. From the age of fourteen he travelled the world for nine years to compete, and it added discipline to his unconventional skill set. 'If you're a tennis player, or a rower, you can make a mistake and recover from it. But in shooting, it's one hundred targets and if you miss, you can never get it back. In racing I knew there were sixteen corners a lap and I could always come from the back, but in shooting you've got to be disciplined. Early mistakes stay with you the whole tournament.'

His attention to detail came to the fore when he ran Stewart Grand Prix in the 1990s. 'I was like those guys who run corner shops who know where every packet of crisps are, and exactly how many boxes of matches they've sold. Stewart Grand Prix was a corner shop operation in that regard. It was my business, I owned it, and I knew everything about it. When we sold it to Ford no one could take a decision without first referring it up the line to someone in Detroit.'

The other 'advantage' dyslexia gave Sir Jackie was a modesty about asking for help. He knew he couldn't do everything himself so he made sure he hired the very best people to help him. Sometimes, though, he sought outside counsel and has always had the number of someone to call if he was having difficulty reaching a decision. It says something about the man's integrity when you hear who his mentors have been. King Hussein of Jordan – who was a big fan of motor racing – and Lord King, the former chairman of British Airways, were always happy to talk things over with him.

Throughout his career, Sir Jackie's natural charm has opened a lot of doors and he has an enviable ability to bring people and projects together. 'It's really not that difficult to talk to these people,' he says. 'I learnt early on that my success in racing gave me a profile and that meant people would take my calls. It gave me five minutes of people's time and I discovered that they were actually quite flattered to be asked for their opinion.'

He also realised that his name and reputation only opened a door once. 'You're not going to phone these people up to tell them what the weather's like and talk piffle, because if you do that's the end of the relationship. But if there's a reason for you to call, a proposal for them to consider that will be to their benefit, then they listen and you build a relationship.' Sir Jackie then fosters those relationships with old-fashioned thank-you notes and by maintaining a dialogue when others would only call when they needed something. As I say, the man has integrity. 'I also have a philosophy that you should under-promise and over-deliver. If they know that you always call with something useful, something beneficial, they will take your call for ever.'

Stewart's integrity is best exemplified by his commercial relationships with Moët & Chandon and Rolex. I think it's fair to say that when celebrities are asked to endorse a product, there's a suspicion that they'll promote almost anything if the money is right, and as soon as their celebrity wanes, the relationship will quietly cease. By contrast, Sir Jackie's relationship with both companies is now into its fifth decade and he sits on the board of Moët & Chandon.

'They perceive that I'm giving them more in value than they are paying me,' he says modestly. 'At the end of the day, if you're a fake, if you're not working hard enough or you don't deliver, then they won't need you. There are a lot of other people they could ask. I learnt that when I was racing. One year everyone wanted my autograph, the next year the crowd was following Emerson Fittipaldi because he was better than me that year. If I didn't deliver for these companies, they wouldn't pay my salary.'

These days he is also a global ambassador for the Royal Bank of Scotland, and I think it's very telling that one of the people who has replaced King Hussein and Lord King as his mentors is Fred 'the shred' Goodwin, the discredited former RBS chief executive who has been demonised since the near collapse of the bank. Sir Jackie's integrity and loyalty mean he won't jump on the press's bandwagon. 'Everybody is saying he hasn't done a good job, but let me tell you he is one of the biggest brains in the country. The idea that one man can bring down all those banking institutions is ridiculous.'

And the other person Sir Jackie calls if he wants advice is his fellow knight Martin Sorrell who was his first agent at IMG. The two of them are still friends forty years later. You wouldn't stay friends with someone that long if they didn't have integrity. Perhaps it's no surprise that Sir Jackie is also part of one of the longest and most successful marriages of anyone in sport or showbiz. He has been married to Helen for over forty years. He is truly an enduring success.

14

A RIVAL OR A COMPETITOR?

In sport, the role that rivalry plays in success is obvious: if you're in a race with someone, you want to beat them. I think it's human nature to want to be better, faster or stronger than someone else. Competition makes us try harder, which means that rivals make us better competitors. If you look at races where world records are set, it's almost always the case that the line-up consists of the world's best competitors. Ask any Arsenal fan what one of the unmissable matches of the season will be and they will tell you it's the game against their north London rivals Tottenham Hotspur. When rivals play each other, they raise their game. The message is simple:

the better our competitors, the better we become.

Early on in my career in rowing, there was one team you had to beat: the Abbagnale brothers from Italy. They had won back-to-back golds at the Olympics and were the most consistent winners in the sport. The first time I competed against them I was so fired up for the occasion that the pair I was in ended up beating them by about ten seconds! That's how badly I wanted to beat them.

I have my own theory as to how they became so dominant in rowing. Of course they had natural ability, and of course they trained very hard, and maybe the fact that they were brothers gave them an ability to communicate effortlessly, but I think they became the best in the world because they first had to become the best in Italy. Their magic ingredient was rivalry. The Abbagnales were from Naples, a city where rowing is a major sport, and the rivalry between the Neapolitans and teams from Rome and Milan, the two other centres of Italian rowing, meant that their desire to beat their regional rivals was immense. The competition between rowing clubs in Italy is far more intense than it is in the UK. That rivalry turned Italy into a rowing superpower for a few years in the early 1980s.

Of course, rivals aren't always in different countries or different clubs – very often they are sitting at the next desk. There's a reason why sales teams have big white boards on the wall marking up who has sold how much: they know that we are all to a certain extent motivated by competition. What is less well recognised is how much more we are motivated by the success of those closest to us. If your best friend is successful, that is going to affect you more than if a total stranger is. The uncomfortable truth is that most of us actually find it quite hard when our friends become successful: it's why siblings are often so competitive. Who would I rather beat at golf – someone I've never met before, or Matthew Pinsent who I play with regularly? It's Matt of course. I hate it when he wins.

In business, the competition between rival companies might not be as obvious as it is in sport (except, perhaps at annual awards ceremonies), but it is every bit as significant. Take Juice Doctor, one of the businesses I have been involved in for the past few years. We make a different kind of juice drink from those offered by Firefly or Innocent, and we think our drink has qualities that set us apart from the other brands. We might not compete with those companies directly on product, but we do compete with them for shelf space in shops, and for the pounds in consumers' pockets. Just because we launch a new flavour, it doesn't mean that corner shops up and down the country are going to get bigger shelves to stock it. In retail there is a finite amount of space, and if a shopkeeper is going to stock Juice Doctor, it means they're going to have to stop selling something else. This commercial reality forces us to find areas where we can be competitive, and to refine our product so that it appeals to more customers. We use our rivals to differentiate ourselves.

When people start new businesses, they are often encouraged to look at their local area and find a business which isn't currently being provided. The logic is simple: if your town doesn't have a coffee shop and coffee shops are popular in other towns, opening one yourself is likely to produce a profit. It's interesting to me that when people retire from sport and start a business, they more often than not take a different view because sport has trained them to think differently.

People who have played sport look at what is already being offered and find a way to do it better. David Lloyd wasn't the first person to open a health club, but he saw an opportunity to introduce tennis courts into the health club scene and this gave him a competitive edge. In business you often hear people talk about 'first mover advantage' and the benefits of being first in any particular market, but I actually think you can do well by looking at what other people have done and finding ways to improve on what they offer.

Sport teaches you to assess your rivals and identify their weak spots, and if that's your mindset you will find flaws in current business offerings, and those flaws represent opportunity. It's how sports professionals have been trained to think. In sport, you learn to use your rivals to improve yourself: if you see someone try a new technique, you have a go at using it yourself. Our rivals constantly provide examples of what to do, as well as what *not* to do. If we can learn from their mistakes as well as our own, we can make faster progress.

Healthy competition

There is a subtle difference between a competitor and a rival. When Portsmouth and Manchester United play each other in the Premier League, it's just another game. But when United play Manchester City, or Liverpool, it *matters*. Rivals have the ability to get under our skin in ways that competitors can't. Rivals make us try that bit harder, which is why it's no surprise that where you find a successful organisation or individual, you will very often find a rival of similar stature. It's not a coincidence that Roger Federer plays his best tennis against Rafa Nadal. In the 1980s, Daley Thompson kept breaking the world decathlon record because he was pushed so hard by his nearest rival, the West German Jurgen Hingsen. Their personal rivalry ensured that the world record was beaten almost every time they competed against each other.

I see a direct parallel with business in this regard. Take software designers and games manufacturers. It is because their rivals keep bringing out improved versions of applications that they have to keep innovating to compete. Without these rivalries, we wouldn't have the iPhone, the Wii or Windows 7. A worthy opponent is the spur to innovation and determination.

> ❝ If you don't have a worthy opponent, it actually pays to go looking for one. ❞

If you don't have a worthy opponent, it actually pays to go looking for one. There was a situation recently in a town I regularly visit where a sandwich shop which had been in business since I was a kid closed down because another sandwich shop opened up down the road. The owner of the old shop had never had a direct rival before and had probably told himself that no one would open up in opposition to him. Why would they when he had the market? What he didn't realise is that the business of making sandwiches – just like every other industry – had moved on. The new shop offered a greater variety of breads and a spectacular number of fillings for the sandwiches. They also had better customer service. The new shop's owners had assessed the incumbent and had decided he didn't pose much of a threat.

The owner of the original sandwich shop had made the mistake of thinking he didn't have any rivals, but the fact was that the lunchtime sandwich trade had moved on from cheese and pickle sandwiches: he didn't realise that his rivals were in other towns. Obviously, no one's going to drive to another town just to buy a sandwich, but by not knowing about the innovations that shops in other towns were making, he lost his business.

A friend of mine runs a hotel. It's been in his family for a couple of generations and it's a very well-known local landmark and it's been a pretty successful business. However, he's just found out that a Premier Inn is going to open within a mile of his premises. Although he's quite scared about the competition and the marketing budget an organisation like Premier Inn has, he's not too daunted. He says it now makes it easier for him to see what he offers the market – personal touches, well-trained staff, fantastic food. With an attitude like that, I think he'll do well.

A rival is the best way I know to guard against complacency. In my career, I could have got away with doing a lot less training if there hadn't been other guys in the squad desperate to take my place in the boat. And it was the fact that there were so many crews in the world that were only fractions of a second slower than we were that kept me training hard. If there hadn't been a threat at every race that someone had been training harder than we had, we would have spent more time on the golf course than we did in the gym.

Complacency is often the biggest challenge that a dominant company, or a dominant team, faces. There have been so many examples in sport of champions being toppled by minnows because they completely underestimated the threat. When I look at the career of really successful people, I see that none of them made the mistake of thinking they were invincible. They always maintained respect for their rivals and, crucially, they kept analysing the competition for threats. Rivals don't take your business, they *make* your business.

> **Case study**
> Name: Sir Richard Branson
> Business: The Virgin Group
> Years in business: 38

Richard Branson is another fellow dyslexic, and like many of us, he found the academic side of school tough. This meant that – despite his middle-class background and public school education – he was never going to be part of the establishment.

He started his entrepreneurial career buying records cheaply abroad and then selling them at boot sales in the UK. This quickly became a record shop and he used the profits from the shop to start his own record label. He famously called his company Virgin because he didn't know much about the record industry. That didn't seem to matter: his label's first release was Mike Oldfield's *Tubular Bells* which became an enduring hit. In the years that followed, acts like the Sex Pistols and Culture Club were signed to Virgin.

It came as a bit of surprise when, in 1984, Branson announced he was launching an airline. After all, there's not much in common between the two industries. Branson had been approached by a new company that wanted financial backing to take over the transatlantic route previously used by the failed Laker airlines. Branson liked the idea so much he didn't want to back the venture, he wanted to run it. 'My interest in life comes from setting myself huge, apparently unachievable, challenges and trying to rise above them,' he said in his autobiography. He intended to bring a little bit of showbiz glamour to the drudge of flying. In doing so, he went head-to-head with British Airways, and one of the greatest rivalries in British business got underway.

I've already talked about how, in sport, your rivals give you a benchmark to measure yourself against. Branson knew he could not compete with BA on size – they had hundreds of aircraft, operated hundreds of routes and employed thousands of staff – so he competed on service and offered in-flight entertainment and comfort that outclassed most other carriers of the day.

Aviation is a regulated industry, and at the time the only British carrier with routes to America from Heathrow was BA. Virgin was forced to fly from London's second airport, Gatwick, to New York's second airport, Newark. Given that Virgin Atlantic only had one plane to start with, you wouldn't think that BA – which branded itself the world's favourite airline – would have been too worried about its new competitor. But as Virgin grew, so did the animosity between the two companies.

In 1991, thanks to lobbying from airline owners like Branson, BA's monopoly on Heathrow routes was ended. When the Civil Aviation Authority granted landing slots for Tokyo flights to Virgin, King called it 'a confiscation of [BA's] property'. There was an obvious culture clash between King and Branson, and it seemed to outsiders that their rivalry had become personal.

At times things got petty between the two firms. When BA stopped using a Union Jack design on their tail fins, Virgin was quick to emblazon their planes with the flag, along with the slogan 'the nation's flag carrier'. Things got a little more serious, however, during the infamous 'dirty tricks affair' where BA had to admit a two-year campaign of evidence gathering against Virgin. When the story broke, both companies counter-sued for libel and ended up in court. BA lost and was ordered to pay Branson £500,000 in damages which he distributed among Virgin Atlantic staff.

If BA had hoped the recession of the early 1990s would be enough to scupper its upstart rival, the news that Branson had sold Virgin Records to EMI for a reported $1bn meant he had deep enough pockets to see Virgin Atlantic through for the long term. If it was hoped the rivalry would subside with a change of personnel at BA, new chief executive Bob Ayling revealed that Branson's encroachment on traditional BA turf was taking its toll. 'This is an airline. I am not going to open a bank. I'm not going to launch clothing shops. I'm not going to be dressing up in bridal gear. I'm not going to be wearing make-up,' he said, making an obvious dig at Branson who had by then diversified the Virgin brand into numerous industries. 'I don't think stunts are the way to manage a company.'

In 2006 a new story surfaced: Virgin tipped off the US and UK competition authorities about price-fixing attempts between Virgin and BA on transatlantic routes. Virgin was given immunity from prosecution, and BA was landed with a £271m fine. Branson summed up the relationship between the companies with this understatement: 'We've always had a pretty competitive and pretty ferocious battle with British Airways . . . we're very pleased to have survived it.'

Like all good rivals, BA helped to make Virgin Atlantic better. At launch, it gave it a benchmark to set itself against, as well as something to rail against. And as the business grew, the rivalry gave them the desire to prove themselves and win whenever the two companies went head to head. Just as sporting rivalries result in world records, business rivalries seem to result in better companies.

Branson's competitive streak is clearly evident in his adventurous attempts to fly non-stop round the world in a balloon, or offer the first commercial flights into space. His commercial nous has been proven in fields as disparate – and random – as gyms, mobile phones and vodka. But whether you look at his ventures that were comparative flops – Virgin Brides or Virgin Vodka – or even his successes like Virgin Money and Virgin Media, nothing compares to the success he has had running Virgin Atlantic. I can't help wondering how much of that is due to the impact of his rivalry with BA.

15

THE ART OF REINVENTION

In the early 1990s, British Rowing employed a new head coach. Jurgen Gröbler had previously been in charge of the East German rowing team, but after the fall of the Berlin Wall, he was able to move to the UK.

The success of the Eastern Bloc countries in rowing had been controversial. There had been persistent rumours about doping, but the thing that really made a difference was that the East German athletes were training full-time. Officially they were employed by the state as police officers or soldiers, and this meant they had a full-time salary while they trained, full-time, with Jurgen. In Britain, I was one of the very few rowers who saw my sport as a full-time occupation, and financially I paid the price for that. Most of my colleagues had salaried jobs outside the sport. When rowers in Britain received a pittance in grants and were expected to pay to compete, it's understandable that there was some resentment expressed about the East Germans. Jurgen's arrival was always going to create a bit of a stir, but we were in for a shock when we realised just how much he intended to change things.

Before Jurgen, the targets for British rowing were based on achieving ninth place or better in the major championships. There was an annual event in Nottingham where British crews competed against each other, and boats that could match the ninth fastest time in the world that year were eligible for funding.

What Jurgen realised was that this effectively meant that success in British rowing meant not even qualifying for major finals, as there are only six boats in a race. His reasoning was that we were actually training to fail. What Jurgen proposed was a complete reinvention of the way we trained. He analysed the winning times achieved at major championships over the past couple of decades, and by looking at the rate of improvement in those times, he was able to predict the time the gold medallists would have to produce at the next tournament. The ambition was no longer to come ninth or better. It wasn't even to match the best time in the world, it was to match the best *future* time in the world.

In reality, Britain had been winning gold medals before Jurgen's arrival. Although the rowing authorities might have been happy with ninth place, competitors like Andy Holmes and myself and our previous coach Mike Spracklen were never going to be satisfied with anything less than gold. Nevertheless, we quickly felt the impact Jurgen's new thresholds had on our training. Jurgen professionalised our systems, and it wasn't just my results that improved. By reinventing our training programmes, he made an enormous impact on the success of the British team.

Mike and Jurgen are probably the two best rowing coaches in the world, but there was something about Jurgen's arrival that invigorated British rowing. I came to the conclusion that change is the antidote to complacency. Change keeps things interesting. When Matthew Pinsent and I decided after Atlanta in 1996 that we were going to carry on for another four years – despite what I may have said to the press about shooting me if I ever went near a boat again – we needed to do something different to keep it interesting. We had been rowing in a pair for six or seven years and we knew everything there was to know about rowing and competing with one another. Moving into a four and having two other guys in the crew, was the change we needed to maintain our levels of enthusiasm.

When I look at other people who have also enjoyed long careers, I see that most of them have also been spurred on by a certain amount of reinvention. In pop music, reinvention is frequently cited as the key to long-term success, whether it's Madonna changing her image, or Sir Paul McCartney releasing experimental tracks as The Fireman. Indeed, Sir Richard Branson may still be leading the Virgin Group, but his collection of businesses – an airline, a bank, a train company, a broadband provider – has little to do with his original business of running a record label. I imagine he would have got bored if he hadn't diversified. And if you look at the Dragons from *Dragons' Den*, you see that they are all serially successful: Peter Jones started running a tennis academy and now runs a telecoms business; Duncan Bannatyne made his fortune in the care home industry before opening his health clubs; James Caan ran a series of recruitment agencies before moving into private equity. It seems to me that reinvention is a key component of enduring success.

Change or die

When organisations fail to respond to changes in their customers' needs, to changes in the economy or to shifts in fashion, they become vulnerable. One of the best examples of the need to change is the fate of Marks and Spencer. M&S is one of the best-known shops on the high street, possibly the best-known, and for years it was able to pull people in off the street with its dependable clothing designs. In the 1990s, M&S believed its long history (the first branch opened in 1884) and its role as the nation's best-known retailer meant it was invincible. And what happened? It's share price dropped by more than 60 per cent and its profits slumped by hundreds of millions of pounds.

The general consensus was that customers had begun to see M&S as a company that was stuck in the past. It didn't take credit cards in an age when plastic had become the first choice for many shoppers, and its designs had drifted from 'classic' to 'dated'. The board realised that if Marks and Spencer didn't change, its days were numbered. A new chief executive was hired, new designers were employed and the business was rebranded in marketing material as 'Your M&S'. A few years into the new century, M&S seemed like a completely different store, so much so that its handful of loyal shoppers now felt that the new style M&S didn't cater for them. They might have been disappointed, but the shareholders weren't: profits started to climb, and so did the share price.

M&S's reinvention was imposed on it. It was a case of 'change or die', but Branson's successive reinventions of the Virgin empire have had different roots. After successes making records with Virgin Records and selling them through Virgin Megastores, Richard Branson decided he wanted to start an airline. The aviation and record industries don't have a lot of obvious similarities, but Branson was very astute in taking the Virgin brand – a slightly anarchic, fun, positive brand – and using it to shake up the corporate world of aviation. Not only did he create an airline that people positively chose to fly with because of its in-flight entertainment, but he also established that the Virgin brand could be applied to anything. If customers responded to the Virgin brand in one arena, why wouldn't they if Virgin started a subsidiary in another area? Ever since, Virgin's new businesses aren't seen as departures, but as extensions of the brand.

I don't suppose Richard Branson realised it at the time, but by constantly changing what Virgin did, he was ensuring his company's longevity. If he had never moved into new sectors, he wouldn't be a billionaire: Virgin Records was sold to EMI, a company which has recently reported huge financial losses; and Virgin Megastores disappeared from our high streets when sales of CDs gave way to downloads. If Virgin hadn't changed, it wouldn't exist.

> " Sometimes quite small changes can bring about significant but subtle reinvention. "

Reinvention doesn't always have to be quite so dramatic. Sometimes quite small changes – like Jurgen's gold times – can bring about significant but subtle reinvention. Take Tiger Woods. He is undoubtedly the most successful golfer of his generation, yet at a time when he was at his most dominant in the sport, he did something remarkable: he changed his technique. He fixed what wasn't broke. He realised that the way he was playing golf would shorten his career so he unlearnt twenty years of training, and found a new way to hit a golf ball. For a while his performance suffered, even though to the average sports fan he wasn't doing anything dramatically different. But then it clicked. His muscles learnt just how to hold themselves and he was able once again to drive the power from his shoulders into the ball and send it with accuracy to the other end of the fairway. Tiger Woods' reinvention was so subtle that fans watching on TV barely noticed it, yet it is the reason why commentators predict that – despite the turmoil in his private life – he will one day break Jack Nicklaus's record for major victories.

One of my favourite stories of reinvention is that of the high jumper Dick Fosbury, a one-man revolution. As a teenage athlete, Dick Fosbury was barely average as a high jumper. His personal best was 5ft 4ins, which is a damn sight higher than I could jump, but still a way off the world record of 7ft 4ins. For most people, this might have been the cue to take his studies more seriously, but instead of focusing on his academic career, Fosbury stayed on his college's athletics field to experiment with different techniques. In the early 1960s, the favourite high-jump technique was the straddle jump, where the jumper went face down over the bar, although many competitors still favoured the traditional scissor jump. By the end of the decade, the only athletes who won high-jump competitions were doing what would become known as the Fosbury Flop.

How on earth Dick Fosbury worked out that if you took a longer run at the high jump, twisted round on a vertical take-off, and then went head first over the bar backwards it would enable you to jump higher, I cannot imagine, but that is exactly the technique he devised. His personal best went from 5ft 4ins to 7ft 4ins and in 1968 he won Olympic gold. Traditionalists were so shocked by what he could do that there were demands for Fosbury to be banned from competition.

There are very few people in history who can claim

to have revolutionised their field, to have turned something – in his case almost literally – on its head and transform the results everyone was capable of achieving. If Fosbury hadn't stayed out there on his college's athletics field and practised as hard as he did, it is possible that the straddle jump would still be the preferred technique of high jumpers. Sometimes it takes one person working quietly on their own to realise something the rest of us have been too busy to work out. It makes you wonder, doesn't it, what improvements we could all achieve in our own lives and businesses if we reassessed our techniques as methodically as Dick Fosbury did.

Case study
Business: Apple Inc. consumer electronics
Years in business: 34

Personal computers are now so central to our lives that it is hard to imagine life without them. Yet at some point in the early 1970s, a group of young guys on America's west coast, did the opposite: they imagined a future *with* computers. First, however, they had to imagine the computer itself. Two of those 'imagineers' were Steve Jobs and Steve Wozniak who had met at

Hewlett Packard (then a manufacturer of mainframe computers for large organisations and office equipment). They also attended the now famous Homebrew Computer Club where members built computers from scratch with whatever equipment they could find or make.

Of the two Steves, Wozniak was the technical genius who went on to build the first Apple computers by hand in the other Steve's parents' garage. Those first computers look nothing like the sleek designs Apple is known for today: they were sold in kit form and didn't even come with a screen or a keyboard, or even a housing unit – they were just a series of motherboards that needed to be connected together. The two Steves, along with an older friend Ronald Wayne who helped set up the company, found their kits sold better than expected and they looked around for investors so they could expand. Wayne, who had kids and a mortgage, decided it was too risky a venture for him to be involved in, and he gave his shares back to the two Steves for $800. Wozniak and Jobs found a new partner, Mike Markkula, who was willing to put in $250,000 and they went into production with their Apple II computer.

Apple was different from the other computer companies that formed in the 1970s for a couple of reasons. The first was the personality of Steve Jobs. A Buddhist who had experimented with LSD, he wasn't interested in becoming 'corporate'. The second reason was the fact that Apple made hardware as well as the software for their computers. Every other company either made one or the other. This contributed to Apple having a reputation for being different, which in turn meant their computers were shunned by corporations who needed computers to be compatible with their clients' computers. However, Apple computers were embraced by the creative industries and over the next few years Apple grew to become a multimillion-dollar company.

By 1984, computers had stopped being something that companies used, and had started to become the kind of purchase that individuals made, and it was at this point that Apple reinvented the personal computer with the launch of their first Macintosh, a computer that seems dull and clunky now, but was the pinnacle of design and technology back then. Apple announced its intention to grab the domestic market with one of the most ambitious TV ads ever made. Directed by Ridley Scott, it depicted an Orwellian 1984-style world of drudgery, gloom and conformity that was smashed with the colour and optimism of Mac. The ad had a budget of $1.5m – a record at the time – and debuted during the

Super Bowl. Pretty much overnight, no one wanted a PC anymore, they wanted an Apple Mac.

The years after the launch of the Macintosh should have been bountiful for Apple, but the second half of the 1980s saw the company lose direction. After a power struggle with John Sculley who had been brought in as CEO from PepsiCo, Steve Jobs left Apple. Steve Wozniak had already left the company in 1987, which meant Apple was now a business without its founders.

Perhaps as a consequence it pretty much lost its identity. One failed launch followed another as the company tried the market in digital cameras, portable CD players, video consoles and speakers, none of which sold sufficiently well. Revenues tumbled, as did the company's share price. Only a spectacular reinvention could save the company now. And of course, that's exactly what happened.

Steve Jobs returned to Apple in 1997 as CEO and oversaw the launch of the most radical personal computer we had ever seen – the iMac. Designed by Brit Jonathan Ive, the iMac revolutionised what we thought a computer could look like. Previously, computers had come in two colours – grey and beige – and had not looked that different from the cardboard boxes they had been shipped in. The iMac was curvaceous, translucent and turquoise. Everything from its keyboard to its mouse to its CD drive had been completely reimagined: Jobs and Ive had managed to create a design classic. Just as companies like Alessi had turned humble kitchen utensils into 'must-have' items, Apple's iMac was coveted for its design as much as its functionality.

It was also Apple's cheapest computer for over a decade. It's no wonder that the iMac sold nearly a million units in its first six months. The thing that had always made Apple different – its anti-corporate image – was now its most valuable selling point. The iMac duly returned Apple to profit and gave the company renewed confidence in itself. For the next couple of years, Apple kept bringing out one beautiful computer – two words never previously linked together – after another.

In the Redgrave household – which I confess is not the most technically advanced – my kids no longer asked for a computer for Christmas, they wanted an iMac. Then, in 2001, Apple unleashed a product that everyone wanted – the iPod. Another stunning design from Jonathan Ive meant that commuters no longer had to carry several CDs to play in their Walkman: the iPod held thousands of tracks digitally and it was small enough to fit into your pocket.

The iPod – along with iTunes, the site that sells tracks to download – was another reinvention for the company that had become known for innovation.

Apple was no longer just a computer company, it was a consumer electronics company. As well as the iPod, it moved into television with Apple TV and telephony with the iPhone. Its latest product, the iPad, looks set to revolutionise electronic publishing and gaming.

Apple's brand is now synonymous with reinvention and that means it could take its brand values of fantastic design, cutting-edge technology and fun and apply them to almost any product. Who knows what they'll do next.

16

GETTING KNOCKED DOWN, GETTING BACK UP

In the careers of almost every person who has achieved enduring success, there will have been a moment where most people – most sane people – would have given up. In the case of some of the entrepreneurs featured in this book, the point when most of us would have given up was when they sold their first businesses for millions of pounds. Why would you carry on working when you've got enough money for the rest of your life? The fact that they can't face retirement says a lot about them. Mostly, however, not giving up means overcoming adversity. It means pushing heavy objects up steep hills. It means a superhuman will to succeed when circumstances seem hell-bent on thwarting you.

You could argue that it takes either a genius or an idiot to start a new business that threatens to bankrupt your existing businesses (as Rupert Murdoch did with Sky), or to put your own money into a manufacturing venture that has been turned down by banks and industry experts (as James Dyson did with his cyclone cleaner), but where most people see barriers, successful people merely see obstacles. Whatever the problem, they have an inner belief that a solution will be found.

I certainly had to rely on my inner belief when, in my rowing career, my health affected my performance. I have written elsewhere about my battles with colitis – a debilitating inflammation of the gut – and diabetes, but for some reason, even though medical experts advised me to retire, I felt I had to carry on. I had to know what I was capable of. There were many, many moments where most people would have given up, but there was only one moment when I seriously considered it.

That was in 1997, three years before the Sydney Olympics and a year after my diagnosis with diabetes. The illness was simply draining me of energy and the power and strength that had made me a great rower had deserted me. My body simply could not compete any more, and when I was at a training camp in South Africa with the British rowing team, the gap between me and the other guys who wanted to compete in Sydney was so great that I realised I didn't deserve to be there. Rowing had been my life and my identity, and the realisation that it had come to an end – not on a podium with a medal round my neck, but in agony and isolation in a nondescript hotel room – added mental anguish to my physical pain. I called my wife at home and told her I didn't think I could go on. I couldn't deal with the diabetes as well as the colitis.

'Don't worry,' she said. 'We'll get through this. We'll find an answer.'

The fact that my wife – who I knew had wanted me to retire after my fourth Olympics – wasn't telling me to get on a plane and come home made me realise that I wasn't alone, and that gave me enough strength to decide I would fight the illness. On my return to the UK, I was incredibly lucky to find a specialist who thought it was possible to compete in an endurance sport with diabetes – I have since found out that he is probably the only diabetes expert in the UK who would have given me that advice – and my medication was altered so that it wouldn't inflame the colitis, and would allow me to carry on. If I hadn't called Ann that day from South Africa, if I had spoken to one of the team instead, maybe I would have been told: 'You're right, it's time to stop.' I wonder what I would have said in response . . .

Nothing in my business career has been as bad as that day in South Africa, but the inner belief I acquired from sport has certainly helped me endure a series of setbacks with one of my businesses when I suspect others less accustomed to knock-backs would have walked away.

When I got involved in Juice Doctor, it seemed to me a relatively straightforward business: we wanted to make juices that rehydrated athletes – and tired shoppers – more efficiently than water by making them isotonic. There are several isotonic drinks on the market, but they all contain additives: Juice Doctor drinks were going to be entirely natural. All we had to do was make the drinks and get them in the shops. How hard could it be?

We brought in a nutritionist to devise the recipes, and she agreed to be paid with shares in the company as there was not enough cash in the business to pay her her normal fee. We then had several tasting sessions, and ran into our first hurdle. There was very little consensus over the recipes. Most were of the 'love 'em or hate 'em' variety, and we needed something that would appeal to more people. So the nutritionist reformulated the recipes, and another round of tasting sessions was undertaken. After a fair bit of trial and error, we settled on three flavours to launch with, one of which was pomegranate. (The reason why I remember pomegranate over the other flavours was that a) it was our most popular flavour, and b) after a few months of operation, we realised that it wasn't profitable. Pomegranate juice was so expensive to produce, that it meant we couldn't be competitive on price. It was a blow, but not a fatal one.)

Our next challenge was getting the juices made and although finding a factory to make them was quite straightforward, we got a very brutal introduction into contract law. The contract was so complicated that I think many people would have torn it up in frustration, but we didn't, and we finally went into production in 2003.

Of course, there's no point having a product if you can't sell it, so the next challenge was distribution. Matt Crane, one of the founders, had previously worked for Safeway so he knew all about getting products into supermarkets. The only problem was that he thought we should avoid the big four supermarkets and maybe target one. His reasoning made sense, however: supermarkets use their buying power to force suppliers to lower their prices – sometimes the margins suppliers make is just 2 or 3 per cent – and we couldn't afford to operate on those margins until we could get the juices made in greater quantities which would reduce their unit price. We targeted one of the big four and over time we landed Sainsbury's. With the other supermarkets out, we decided to approach local independent stores, but instead of having four meetings with the buyers of the big four supermarket chains, this meant taking to the streets and meeting individual shop owners face to face. Even when they agreed to carry Juice Doctor, they would put in an order for just a handful of bottles.

We thought an obvious market for us was schools. After all, surely teachers and parents would rather that pupils drank a healthy juice drink with no additives rather than fizzy pop, but because of the fruit content, the natural sugar content of Juice Doctor drinks is quite high, and that means our drinks can no longer be sold in schools. There are some things you are never going to know until you walk slap bang into them, and in the case of Juice Doctor, we got quite a few bruises running into obstacles.

Nevertheless, we found ways to grow the business and slowly got big enough to target the supermarket chains we'd had to avoid early on. Although we are now stocked in the big four chains, it's still a difficult balancing act at times. However, every time we get stocked in a new outlet, or we are able to increase production and decrease unit costs, we get a little stronger as a company. We have been given countless reasons to throw in the towel since we launched, but the five of us still believe in the business and it's going to take more than a few obstacles to stop us.

Take responsibility

There is a saying that failure is a great teacher, and judging by the number of successful entrepreneurs who have previously lost money on earlier ventures, there's probably some truth in it. For some people, failing in a venture they have put their heart and soul into is a blow from which they find it hard to recover, for others it is an opportunity to fight back. I don't think you can underestimate the power of 'I'll show you'. I have been in races where crews who have been written off by the pundits have been so determined to prove the naysayers wrong that they've put in the performance of their lives. I think it's fairly natural that someone who has just failed in a business venture would want to prove that although the business was a failure, they weren't. For a dyslexic like me who found school a struggle, there was a definite incentive to prove I could succeed outside of the school's academic framework. Fellow dyslexic Sir Jackie Stewart believes his dyslexia is actually the reason for his success in sport and business: he knew he wasn't stupid and he had to find a way to prove it. David Lloyd believes that playing tennis prepared him for the everyday failures he encountered in his business career: you can't play sport unless you are prepared to lose, and so sport teaches you how to learn from failure.

Whenever I lost a race, I wanted to know why. If the race had been filmed I wanted to watch the footage and see if I could identify the point in the race where we had lost. I would analyse everything from the meals I had eaten in preparation to the number of hours I had put into training in a bid to identify the area where I needed to improve. Had I let my nerves get the better of me? Had my tactics been wrong? I was forensic in my analysis: something good had to come out of losing.

Entrepreneurs I have spoken to have said the same thing. Very often businesses that failed weren't bad businesses, sometimes in fact, they were very good businesses, but if one aspect of them was badly managed, then they would falter. It's even possible for profitable businesses to go under if they don't get their cash flow right.

One key attribute that successful people share is a willingness to take responsibility for their failures. Some people will blame the market, or their product manu-facturer, or the supplier who wouldn't give them a better price, or the customers who were too slow to settle invoices. But these are the same people who don't see the difference between identifying the reasons behind a failure, and taking responsibility for those reasons. The truly great operators don't blame anyone else except themselves. Ask them the reason why a venture failed and they will say: 'I failed.'

> " Accepting that there were things you could have done better is the best way of ensuring that you will do those things to a higher standard in the future. "

Blaming third parties for failure means you don't properly learn from setbacks. Accepting that there were things you could have done better is the best way of ensuring that you will do those things to a higher standard in the future. Of course, once you have analysed why a business venture went wrong, it's impossible not to imagine how things would have turned out if you hadn't made those mistakes. Which probably explains why successful people's response to failure is to get back up, dust themselves down and start all over again.

> **Case study**
> Name: Sir James Dyson
> Business: Dyson domestic appliances
> Years in business: 24

The career of Sir James Dyson – Britain's best-known inventor – is a catalogue of problems and failures, but that hasn't stopped him joining the billionaire's club. In his early career, he invented and developed a series of products that didn't quite capture the world's imagination: a ballbarrow (instead of a wheelbarrow) and a water-filled garden roller. Then, in 1979, he bought a top-of-the-range vacuum cleaner and realised it didn't matter how much money you spent on one, it would always lose suction as the bag filled up. He decided to try and invent a vacuum cleaner that didn't lose suction.

On a visit to a local sawmill, he noticed that sawdust was expelled by a fan that sucked the air up like a cyclone. Perhaps, he thought, he could use cyclones to suck dust out of carpets. What happened next has been very well documented. Dyson spent five years working on prototypes in his cellar while the family lived off his wife's salary as a teacher. Five years is a long time to work on a prototype: these days we've been accustomed to near-instant rewards, and it must have seemed even longer because it wasn't just one prototype – it was 5,127.

Let me repeat that number: 5,127. 'I wanted to give up almost every day,' he says now. 'There were times I thought, God, I'm never going to get there. I'm going to go bankrupt. A lot of people give up when the world seems to be against them, but that's the point when you should push a little harder.' As a teenager, Dyson had done a lot of long-distance running and he says he learnt determination from it. 'It seems as though you can't carry on, but if you just get through the pain barrier, you'll see the end and be OK. Often, just around the corner is where the solution will happen.' The big difference between sport and business, however, is that in sport you know where the finish line is. 'I always thought it was just around the corner,' he says. That optimism kept him going.

When he finally had a working prototype, he faced his next two setbacks. The first – getting the necessary patents – wasn't as tough as the second, which was selling his idea to a manufacturer.

You might think that if a manufacturer hears a pitch from an inventor for a product which would sell to pretty much every home in the country, their eyes might light up with £££ signs, especially when that product is demonstrably better than current offerings.

What James Dyson hadn't banked on was that manufacturers wanted to protect the revenues they earned from bag sales. Put simply, a bagless vacuum cleaner meant smaller profits.

To get his cyclone cleaner made, he had to use the same ingenuity he had needed to make the prototype. Having tried all the domestic manufacturers, Sir James had to look abroad. He eventually found a Japanese company that was willing to pay a licence fee to him for using the technology, and in 1986, the first Dyson went on sale in Japan with a price tag of £2,000. At the time, you could buy a Hoover for under £50.

At that price, sales were hardly at the level that makes you think you're going to become a billionaire, but the deal did provide Dyson with a modest income, and perhaps more crucially, a great deal of confidence. The Japanese deal proved that there was a demand for better products. He used the Japanese money to set up his own production facility near his home in Wiltshire. In 1993, he launched his first cyclone cleaner in the UK. Even though it cost £200 – four times the price of a traditional vacuum cleaner – it became the nation's best-selling cleaner just two years later.

The reason for this phenomenal success wasn't just because a Dyson sucked up more dust than its rivals. A Dyson also had a stair hose that actually stretched to the top of the stairs, it cleaned edge-to-edge, and it had a clear bin so you could see when it needed emptying, as well as a carry handle and easy-to-reach attachments. All simple innovations that made vacuum cleaning or as we should maybe now call it, Dysoning, easier as well as better. And of course, because he had been forced to manufacture the cleaners himself, he wasn't sharing the profits with anyone else.

These days, the Dyson company is still innovating with its 'air blade' hand dryers and blade-free desk fans, but the company still makes a lot of mistakes. And that's the way James Dyson likes it. 'I made 5,127 prototypes of my vacuum before I got it right. There were 5,126 failures. But I learnt from each one. That's how I came up with a solution. You start with a problem you want to solve, and you build prototypes to do that. From then, it's a journey from prototype to prototype until you reach the solution. You get hundreds, or thousands, of failures.

'The failure is the starting point because when something fails, you can understand why it fails, and then you can start to think of ways you can overcome that failure. The moral of the tale is, keep on failing.'

You could say that Sir James is passionate about failure. He works with the Design Museum and with schools to encourage would-be inventors to try things out. 'I don't mind failure. I've always thought that schoolchildren should be marked by the number of failures they've had. The child who tries strange things and experiences lots of failures to get there is probably more creative.'

Sir James's story is an inspiration to those people in business – and in life – who keep being knocked down, or who get knocked back, by industries and companies that have an interest in playing safe. His story also highlights the problem of playing safe, as all those manufacturers who turned him down in the 1980s have seen sales of Dysons eclipse every other make of vacuum cleaner in the UK (as well as in several other countries around the world). Put another way, because they weren't prepared to fail, they missed the opportunity to succeed.

17

PUTTING IN THE HOURS

If this was a book about attaining success rather than retaining it, there would almost certainly be a chapter called 'luck'. I consider myself incredibly lucky to have gone to a school where the English master had a passion for rowing that he was committed to sharing with his pupils. If it wasn't for him, my life would have been very, very different. Most of the people in this book were helped by being in the right place at the right time, or of benefiting like I did from a fortuitous encounter. Luck can definitely open doors, but it cannot sustain a career.

It was the great South African golfer Gary Player who famously said 'the harder I work, the luckier I get' and I don't know anyone who would disagree with him.

When successful people have had several 'lucky breaks' in their career, I would argue that their luck is a consequence of their hard work. Initial success means they are more likely to meet people who will help on future ventures. In that regard, luck can breed more luck, but it can only be sustained if, between those lucky breaks, the individuals concerned work hard, deliver the goods and impress the people around them. The way to stay lucky is to work hard.

When I look at the most successful people I know in sport, they have all trained harder than the less successful people. When I was talking to David Lloyd he told me about the time his brother John was married to Chris Evert. 'John was happy to spend an hour or two out on the court,' he said, 'but Chrissie wouldn't stop. She would train for hours.' That goes some of the way to explaining why Chris Evert won eighteen Grand Slam titles and John, well, didn't.

Talent can only get you so far. Drive and desire can only contribute so much. The only way to fulfil promise and potential is to work at it. I may have had a natural aptitude for rowing, but it was the hours on the water that made me competitive, and it was the hours in the gym that made the difference. People don't seriously expect to be good at sport without practice. Jonny Wilkinson became the best kicker in rugby because he spent more hours than was sane practising. Usain Bolt may be unnaturally talented, but it is the hours of training he has put in that have made him a sprinting phenomenon. Even darts and snooker players have to put in an incredible amount of practice if they want to maintain their form.

Yet in business, many people I meet seem to think that success is supposed to come easily. I tell them stories I hear of entrepreneurs working eighty-hour weeks, sometimes hundred-hour weeks, sleeping in their offices because there just isn't time to go home. Sometimes the long hours are because there isn't money to pay someone else to do the small and tedious tasks. Long after clients, staff and customers have gone home, cash-strapped entrepreneurs are poring over their books. Sometimes the long hours are spent in perfecting their products or their techniques. James Caan, one of the Dragons from *Dragons' Den*, tells a great story about how he revised and refined his sales pitch after every phone call when he was setting up his first business. Just like Jonny Wilkinson practising his kicks, Caan practised his pitch, over and over and over again.

Graft is like a catalyst. It is only when you add graft to talent, drive, opportunity and all the other elements of success that something magical happens. It is through dogged hard work that these disparate elements are forged into something with purpose. Add graft and you get results. Without it, the chances are you get nothing.

The problem with graft is that it is hard, and it is often boring. When you picture your future, you are more likely to imagine those moments on podiums or accepting awards than you are those endless hours spent on rowing machines or packaging up products for delivery at midnight because you can't yet afford to pay someone to do it for you. While the end results of hard work can inspire the imagination, the reality can be so hard and so boring that it actually stifles ambition. Ultimately, it is also exhausting. Duncan Bannatyne wrote in his autobiography that he started to have blackouts at one point in his career. The doctors told him that his body was so desperate for sleep it had to find a way to slow him down.

No secret ingredient

While most people are prepared to work hard *some* of the time, people who achieve enduring success are prepared to work hard *most* of the time. Getting a business off the ground doesn't happen in a few days or even a few weeks. In all likelihood it doesn't take months either – it takes years. And if you are working seven days a week and fourteen hours a day (or longer) for years, other areas of your life are going to suffer. To succeed in your chosen field means turning down invites to events you would really like to go to – like friends' weddings and kids' school plays – and missing out on all sorts of cultural events that the rest of the world knows about but that pass you by. Many successful people will tell you that their relationships with friends and family suffered while they put the hours in to make their venture successful. Whether it's cutting out watching TV soap operas or reading newspapers or books, or never seeing your beloved team play another match, sacrifices are required. It's just not possible to do all the normal day-to-day things *and* work extraordinarily hard. Hard work involves making a choice.

> The right amount of hard work can make up for shortfalls elsewhere.

However, the great thing about graft is that we are all capable of doing it – it is not a secret ingredient known only to the initiated. The right amount of hard work can make up for shortfalls elsewhere. Less talented athletes can become champions through the right training. Averagely gifted entrepreneurs can build big and successful businesses by putting in the hours. If you could imagine this book represented on a graph with each of the chapters having their own column, the people who achieve enduring success would score something in each column. But people with a poor showing in the talent column or the vision column or the communication column could still achieve great and lasting success if their score in the graft column is high enough.

In my public speaking, I have found that there are two responses to finding out that hard work can transform an average person, or an average company, into something exceptional. The first response is – and this still surprises me – disappointment. There are a great many people in the world who would rather believe that success is a gift bestowed on the chosen few rather than something seized through tenacity and willpower. If hard work means anyone can succeed, it also means they can no longer kid themselves that anyone other than themselves is responsible for their underachievement.

Most people, however, respond positively to finding out that the future is there for the taking. This is one area where the example of sport is so helpful. You only have to look at footage of Andy Murray playing in 2007 and then look at his matches in 2008 to see the difference his hard work in the gym made to his confidence, to his ability and to his results. It's harder to illustrate how much of a difference hard graft in business can make, but it can transform your professional life as dramatically as it can change sporting fortunes.

The good news for those who are prepared to put in the hours in the short term is that they will reap the rewards in the long term. Although many people who run businesses could be described as workaholics who wouldn't know what to do with their time if they weren't working, there are others who choose – when their business is sufficiently well established – to employ others to run their businesses on their behalf. Moving from a chief executive role to something more like a chairmanship allows entrepreneurs to steer their businesses without doing the day-to-day implementation – perhaps they are only needed to work a day or two a month. Others, of course, get the opportunity to sell their businesses for the kinds of sums that means they never have to work again.

The majority of the population work around thirty-five hours a week over a career of forty or so years. Over the course of their careers, entrepreneurs probably work a comparable number of hours, it's just that they condense those hours into fewer years. Perhaps that's something to hold on to when you find yourself still at your desk long after everyone else in your business has not just gone home, but gone to bed.

Case study
Name: Peter Jones
Business: Phones International
Years in business: 28

Peter Jones started his first business when he was seventeen. For several summers he had helped a teacher from his school give tennis lessons at a local club. It seems he didn't do much more than collect the balls and carry the rackets, but it says something about him as an entrepreneur that he realised he too could make money out of teaching tennis. As soon as he turned sixteen, he enrolled on the LTA's coaching programme and after he qualified he launched what he called his own tennis 'academy'. He negotiated use of the courts from his local club and advertised for customers. He then hired his own assistant to pick up the balls and carry the rackets so that he could coach more players and earn more money. By using the existing facilities at the tennis club, he didn't need to take out his own insurance, or buy his own kit; in fact his start-up costs were virtually nil. It's not a big business by any stretch of the imagination, but it's got to have been one of the most profitable businesses started by someone who was also studying for their A levels!

He continued his seven-days-a-week schedule when he left school and started work at local computer companies – first working for a software firm and then for a hardware business – while continuing to coach tennis at the weekends. At an age when most teenagers would be spending their mornings in bed and their evenings in the pub, Peter Jones was doing some seriously hard graft.

I am a firm believer that there are only two real ways to make money. The first is luck and the second is graft. Hard work is like the yeast that turns dough into bread, it's the active ingredient that combines all the others to make something bigger and better than its constituent parts. Jones clearly had a lot going for him – he was bright, ambitious and tenacious – but it was his willingness to put in the hours that turned him from a dreamer to a millionaire. By the age of twenty he had enough knowledge of computers, and enough confidence from his tennis academy, to start his own business that built and maintained computer systems for local businesses.

Not long afterwards he was driving a Porsche and living the high life.

I find Peter Jones's story fascinating. He grew up not far from me and is just a few years younger than me, and I want to understand how someone whose background is not that different from my own can create a multimillion-pound fortune from nothing. Unlike some of the other people I've profiled in this book, Peter Jones's story makes me realise that these titans of business aren't very different from everyone else: they just worked harder. I pushed myself in the gym to get the strength to win races just as Peter worked seven days a week to get experience.

In the same way that athletes become so convinced of their own ability that they underestimate the competition, at the age of twenty-six Peter Jones was taught a very painful, but valuable, lesson. 'I'd made many stupid mistakes,' he says in his book *Tycoon*. 'I'd been doing so well that I'd failed to protect the business. I hadn't bothered doing credit checks or insuring the business adequately.' While he'd assumed his business was invincible, his customers were going to the wall. And of course when they didn't pay their invoices, he couldn't pay his. Peter's business went bust, his Porsche was sold and he found himself living in his office. 'It had a desk and bed in it. I had no money, no car and, perhaps even worse, no hot water. Every day for six months I had to wash in cold water. I also spent a few weeks living back with my parents.'

After another failed business running a restaurant and cocktail bar, Jones needed to rebuild his finances, and presumably his confidence, and spent the next few years working for other people and climbing the corporate ladder. But it had always been his ambition to run his own company, and in 1998, he set up Phones International, a distribution company for mobile phone manufacturers. He did deals with the phone companies and then sold their products to retailers.

He certainly wasn't the first person doing this – by 1998 quite a lot of people already had a mobile phone – nor was he the only one. But he entered the market at a tipping point when mobile phones went from being accessories for City types in flash suits, to being something that schoolkids had in their backpacks. The market was about to explode, and Jones saw an opportunity to get a piece of it.

His strategy to deal with his competition was to specialise. He decided to sell only Ericsson phones. He became an expert in their functionality, repair and accessories. Phones International knew more about Ericsson phones than any other distributor and could therefore offer retailers a better service. This meant retailers bought from him rather than his rivals, and Ericsson rewarded his loyalty with better prices. In its first year, Phones International had sales of £13.9m. Some people might look at that figure and think 'jammy git', but I look at it with amazement. For a brand new company in an intensely competitive field to achieve sales of almost £14m is incredible. That can't be luck. That can only be a consequence of hard work.

Over the next few years, sales increased and soon enough the profits were in seven digits, which is the point when many people might decide to start taking things easy. But instead Jones used the money to buy up other companies, one of which he turned around and sold eighteen months later for a huge profit.

In 2005, Jones appeared in the first series of *Dragons' Den*, and over the course of seven series he has invested in several businesses, all of which demand his attention. He has also bought, along with Theo Paphitis, Red Letter Days, an events company that organises special activity days out. And not content with the profile he received from the *Den*, he devised his own version of *Pop Idol* and – along with Simon Cowell – launched *American Inventor* on US television, as well as *Tycoon* on ITV. These shows might not have had the impact of *Dragons' Den*, but they show Peter's willingness and ability to work hard when, frankly, he could afford to spend the rest of his life on a beach in the Caribbean.

Interestingly, since his TV career took off, he says he has had to make himself take more time off. 'Now because I've got even more business interests and things to do, I actually need a holiday,' he says. When he ran his first business, he worried that if he took time off he would lose customers, so he didn't tell people he was away – he didn't even change his voicemail message. The consequence was that when he did leave the office, he was paranoid about the workload that was building up. Technology now means he can combine holidays with work. 'I don't stop when I'm away; the communication lines are always open. I'm on my BlackBerry at certain times of the day, so it's like I'm working from home for a few weeks. Even on holiday I do not switch off from my business completely.' For the enduringly successful, the hard work never stops.

18

THE 50 PER CENT RULE

As well as talking to businesses and corporations, I also attend a lot of events in schools. Getting involved in sport at school changed my life, and I'm always keen to do whatever I can to get youngsters to try as many sports as possible. After all, how do you know if you'll have a talent for, say, throwing a discus, bowling offspin or sailing unless you try it?

My dyslexia meant I found school boring. I was lucky in that I was always big and so I wasn't made fun of in the way that other kids were, but I knew I wasn't doing well in lessons and it was incredibly demoralising. The idea of sitting exams or, worse, sitting in an office doing paperwork for the rest of my life filled me with dread. Which is why, when I was encouraged to try rowing, my life changed so dramatically. I had found something I was good at, something I was better at than most people, and it did miracles for my self-esteem. When you're good at something, you enjoy it, and unless you enjoy something, you're not going to stick with it.

One of the secrets of enduring success is to find something you love to do – maybe if you're lucky it will be the thing you were born to do – and then see if you can also find a way to make it the thing you do for money. I have never been particularly motivated by money – if I was, I couldn't have stayed in a sport that didn't pay for twenty-five years – but the thought of being better than anyone else at something was so compelling to me that I followed rowing as a career when many others would have found something more lucrative to do.

When I go into schools, I don't go there trying to convince kids to take up rowing. I tell them to find something they love – whether that's an obscure sport, maths or needlework doesn't matter to me. So long as they find something they enjoy doing, I tell them they'll find a way to make a career out of it. I consider myself very lucky to have been able to scrape an income out of the sport I loved, but without my parents' support in the early days, and the grants and sponsorship that became available as time went on, it would have been impossible. Very few of us get the chance to pursue their dream to the extent that I did.

If you can't make a career out of the thing you love doing, the next best option is to love the career you've chosen. In every business, in every job, there are elements that are more or less interesting than others, and some people will enjoy some tasks more than others. Even in my career, following a sport I loved, there were days when I hated it. Those cold dark mornings on the river weren't much fun, and some of the sessions in the gym were mentally as well as physically painful, and of course, there were also the corporate events I had to attend as part of my sponsorship deals. Every job, no matter how satisfying, has its downsides. When you find yourself doing something you don't enjoy, you need to remind yourself why you're doing it. Just like dieting isn't much fun but losing weight is, sometimes you need to focus on the result, not the race.

> Unless you love what you do for at least 50 per cent of the time, then you can't be happy doing all the other aspects of your work that make up the other 50 per cent.

I have a 50 per cent rule. I think that unless you love what you do for at least 50 per cent of the time, then you can't be happy doing all the other aspects of your work that make up the other 50 per cent. Through delegation and good management, it's usually possible to shift that 50 per cent figure closer to 75 per cent, but I don't think it's possible to ever completely eliminate all the bad stuff – there will always be a colleague, a client or an event that you won't like. What I tell kids in schools is that if they're not prepared to put up with a bit of grief, then they don't stand a chance of enjoying the good stuff.

One way to make a bad job better is to do it with people you like and admire. I sometimes wonder if I would have been able to achieve the same level of success in my chosen discipline – the single sculls – as I eventually went on to achieve in rowing as part of a team. I had a vision of myself as a solo sportsman, but I had to face the fact that my results as a solo oarsman weren't world class. Something happened when I started training in a team, and that something made me a better competitor. Looking back, I think it was because I was having more fun.

When I think about how hard I used to train – two or three sessions on the river a day, running from my house to the river to fit in more training, hours in the gym with weights – it's no wonder that sharing that monotony with someone else made it more bearable. As I said earlier, at the time of writing I am training to cycle across America to raise funds for Sport Relief. I have the choice of training in a gym I've installed in my garage, or cycling several miles to train with the guys I will be crossing America with. Guess which one I choose to do? Even though in many ways I am a loner, I still respond positively to being part of a good team. I might not like the music they choose to work out to, but it's a damn sight better than silence!

In the last chapter, I talked about the hard training Andy Murray put in that saw him rise to number three in the world. What I didn't mention was that he also changed his coaching arrangements. Instead of travelling the world with just one coach – something he found pretty dull, and therefore demoralising – Murray decided he needed a team around him. Team Murray are now infamous on the ATP tour for having fun. His coach, his fitness trainers and physio all have nicknames and they have a reputation for playing practical jokes on one another. They also bet on absolutely everything, and the forfeits for losing their bets include wearing pink tracksuits for a week or taking an ice bath. The fact that Murray has fun while he trains means he trains for longer, which in turn means he gets results – and that's something he definitely enjoys.

Getting the balance right

Running a business can also be pretty lonely. There are tough decisions to make that no one else can make, there are presentations to give that no one else in the company can give, and anyone who has started their own business will know how it feels to still be at your desk three or four hours after the last employee has left the office. The thing that enables you to do that is the same thing that enabled me to get on the river in the middle of winter when it was still dark: the dream that all the hard work will amount to something. In these situations, you've got to enjoy your dream. You've got to be able to say to yourself: 'I *will* deal with this abusive customer, or this expensive supplier, because they enable me to make my dream come true.' By focusing on the fun, you can deal with the drudge.

It seems to be a pattern in most industries that the higher up the corporate ladder you get, the more you can eliminate the tedious aspects of your work. Kids starting at the bottom might have to put up with spending more hours on tasks they dislike than the people with experience. It's why Sir Alex Ferguson gets the youth team at Manchester United to clean the first team's boots: if they can see what the end reward is, they can endure the hard slog it will take to get to the top. We are prepared to do the junior jobs because we can see that the reward is promotion to a job where the fun:drudge ratio gets a bit more favourable.

Just as we rationalise that the 'junior' jobs in an organisation will lead to a more senior position as a way to help us cope with the drudgery, we need to find ways at every stage in our careers to view our work more positively. If you're having a bad patch or working for a bad boss, you need to focus on the good aspects of your work.

One of the things that can make a job more enjoyable is when we feel we have a little bit of control. Whether it's being asked for our input or allowed to make our own decisions, jobs where we feel we are useful and valued make us happier. In my public speaking, I encourage people to take ownership of their careers because every time you are aware you are making an active choice, you feel you are in control. Knowing that I was the only person pushing myself that hard in training somehow made it better: nobody forced me.

I also find you can get more out of your work if you care about it. Doing the most menial task can be rewarding if you care about doing it well. Caring whether or not your customer is satisfied is the best way of making sure that they will be satisfied. Caring that your clients are happy or your boss is happy or your colleagues are happy, means that you get pleasure from doing the things that put a smile on their faces, even if those things themselves are hard work.

Another option is to build fun into what you do. I know from my work with Comic Relief that companies that raise funds together report higher levels of staff happiness. Whether people run marathons with their colleagues or sponsor each other to see who can type the fastest, doing things as part of a team is more fun than doing them on your own. Whether it's regular get-togethers in the pub, a company sports day or team-building days out, finding ways for your team to enjoy each other's company means that when they get down to work, they'll be more likely to work hard.

When I look back on my hard days training, do I remember the shivers as I got on to the water? Sure. But do I mostly look back on the day when Matt, Tim and James hid a statue in the bathroom of my hotel room to give me the fright of my life? Or do I relive the time when Matt and I kept swapping Tim and James's car keys over so that they could never work out what was wrong with their central locking system? Funnily enough, as time goes on, it's the fun stuff I remember more, and the more I realise that having fun was just as important to my success as those long, hard hours in a boat.

> **Case study**
> Name: Michael Eavis
> Business: Founder of the Glastonbury Festival
> Years of operation: 40

In 2009, *Time* magazine produced a list of the hundred most influential people in the world. Along with presidents and prime ministers, billionaires and movie stars, was a seventy-three-year-old dairy farmer from Somerset. But then Michael Eavis doesn't just milk cows for a living, he also runs the Glastonbury Festival.

Glastonbury is such an icon of cultural life in Britain that the BBC's coverage of it is on a par with their broadcasts from the Proms, or arguably even Wimbledon. Even though the 'festival season' now starts in May and runs through to September, and despite the statistic that over 3 million tickets were sold for UK festivals in 2008, Glastonbury is still considered special. Which is why pop stars and prime ministers will take Michael Eavis's calls, which in turn is why he is considered so influential.

There are many theories as why Glastonbury remains special. Some people say it is the location, some say it's the music, but pretty much everyone agrees that a little bit of Glasto's magic comes directly from Michael. If he was so minded, Eavis could be a multimillionaire by now, but the profits from his festival are given to charity. At the last Glastonbury in 2009, over £1.3m was donated to Greenpeace and WaterAid, organisations with which Eavis has had a relationship for decades. But that doesn't quite explain why the Glastonbury vibe is significantly less corporate than other festivals. I think the difference comes from the fact that whereas other festivals are run for profit, Michael Eavis runs Glastonbury for fun.

The fortieth anniversary of the first festival on Eavis's Worthy Farm falls in 2010. The 1970 event was a low-key affair that saw around 1,500 music fans pay £1 (which included as much milk as they could drink) to watch Marc Bolan, Keith Christmas, Stackridge and Al Stewart. Although everyone – including Eavis – had a great time, it left him with a £1,500 debt, and that was just the first in a series of setbacks.

By 1979, the festival had become a three-day event, and the losses were so bad that year that no one wanted to back another festival in 1980. It was at this point that Eavis recognised that if he wanted to keep using his farm for a music festival, he was going to have to pay as much attention to the books as to the music. The festival returned in 1981 complete with its iconic pyramid stage (which doubled as an unusual cowshed and food store the rest of the year).

The festival needed to be licensed by the local council for the first time in 1984, and as the festival got bigger, so did the demands from locals for the council to refuse Eavis a licence. The following year, Eavis had to defend himself against five prosecutions brought by the council for breaches of the licence, all of which were dismissed. For every local resident who loved the festival, there was another who hated it for taking over the village.

As the festival got bigger, so did the problems. A perimeter fence had to be installed to stop non-ticket holders getting in, and at 1990's event, there were hundreds of arrests and tens of thousands of pounds worth of criminal damage. It got even worse in 1994 when there was a shooting incident and a reveller died from a drugs overdose.

I think most people, faced with such a catalogue of setbacks, would have thrown in the towel. But then most of us have never experienced the thrill of throwing the biggest party in the world. At each festival, Eavis – whose Abraham Lincoln beard makes him pretty memorable – gets his hand shaken by thousands of smiling music fans who recognise him and want to show their appreciation for his dedication. Most of us don't know what it's like to have huge international superstars calling up for a chat. Nor do many people know the pleasure of raising over a £1m a year for causes they're passionate about.

'I do enjoy myself immensely,' Eavis has said. 'I have a hell of a good time. I've got the best life anyone could possibly have. I'm not moaning. This whole festival thing is better than alcohol, better than drugs.' Contrary to the popular image of festival goers, Glastonbury's founder is a self-confessed puritan. What he does share with the revellers is a love of music. How many people in their seventies can be credited with breaking new bands? And while his choice of headliners is sometimes controversial, it is also frequently inexplicable – although not for long. Chris Martin from Coldplay explained in an article for *Time*: 'Michael is so good at tapping into the zeitgeist months before anyone else. You'll wonder, why are the Kings of Leon headlining this year? Inevitably, six months later Kings of Leon are the biggest thing going.'

Although much of the festival organising has now been handed on to Eavis's daughter Emily, Michael still influences the line-up. Where other people of his generation might be happy to listen to the music they knew when they were younger, Eavis gets a bigger thrill from new music.

Eavis has estimated that the festival takes up about half of his year. The rest of the time he is still a working dairy farmer looking after a herd of 250 Friesians. Although it is said to be one of the most profitable dairy farms in the country, Eavis does not have an extravagant lifestyle. Where his showbiz friends might have mansions in the Hamptons or villas on private islands in the Caribbean, Eavis displays a farmer's practicality when it comes to spending money: 'If I have any money spare, it'll go on a new slurry pit, not a swimming pool or a holiday in Barbados.'

This attitude, combined with the fundraising, is part of the reason why Glastonbury is still seen as different from the other festivals. The pilgrims who find their way to Worthy Farm each summer can have more fun themselves because they know the money they have spent on tickets is not funding a millionaire lifestyle. And of course it's not just the ticket holders that have fun. Coldplay and Sir Paul McCartney headlined Glastonbury for a tiny fraction of their usual fee because they knew they would have fun playing there too. When the founder, the punters and the performers continue to have such a good time, it doesn't sound like the Glastonbury Festival will be ending any time soon.

CONCLUSION

In 2009, Roger Federer and Andy Roddick played in the longest ever Wimbledon final (if you measure it by the number of games played). The score in the fifth set was a gruelling 16–14, and while the tennis might not have been as supreme as Federer's previous Wimbledon final against Rafael Nadal – by common consensus the greatest game of tennis ever played at SW19 (and the longest if you measure in time, a colossal four hours and 48 minutes) – the Roddick final was one of the greatest pieces of sporting theatre I have ever seen.

Both men were desperate to win, but for completely different reasons. For Federer, victory would take him into the history books by eclipsing the record he shared with Pete Sampras for Grand Slam victories. He alone in the world would know what it felt like to win a fifteenth Slam. For Roddick, victory would rewrite his slightly smaller entry in the record books: he would no longer be a 'one Slam wonder', a flash-in-the-pan, the guy who was good enough only once. Roddick clung on for victory like a rock climber gripping an overhanging bluff: he did not want to be an also-ran, a footnote, a fluke.

As I watched, I was pretty sure Roddick would win. The psychology was in his favour: Federer, in the back of his mind, would know that he would have other chances, whereas this was, in all likelihood, Roddick's last throw of the dice. Not only that, but Federer had not broken Roddick's serve. Roddick appeared unbreakable and there was no way he was going to let his chance slip away. But in the end, after more than four and a quarter hours on court, and after just one break of serve, it was Federer who jumped in the air in victory.

I now see it was inevitable that Federer would win. He had talent, perseverance, momentum, drive, and his rivalry against both Sampras's record and Nadal's threat to his world number one status gave him the edge. He had won before and he knew what it took to win again.

Compared to business, sporting careers are inevitably short. Federer only won his first Grand Slam in 2003, but in tennis terms, he has become an enduring success; overcoming a back injury and withstanding the threat from the more powerful Nadal when it seemed the Spaniard was set to dominate the sport. Success doesn't just breed success, it breeds enduring success.

If Andy Roddick was in business, his record would appear much closer to Federer's. They would both feature in 'top ten' lists of the most successful, or the most influential, and the public would find it hard to distinguish the size of Roddick's balance sheet, or his market capitalisation, from that of his rival's. In that regard, sport is harsher than business, but in other ways, attaining enduring success in business takes a kind of stamina not needed in sport.

Ten years is a long sporting career. Twenty years is remarkable. Anything longer than that, I have been fortunate to find out, qualifies you as something of a legend. However, in business a twenty-year career might not even see you to your fortieth birthday. In sport, you may have to face new rivals, but you pretty much always compete on the same sized pitch, the same length of track or the same stretch of water. In business, there are no such comforts: the playing field can be transformed by economic shifts, changes in legislation, and improvements in technology or globalisation bring new competition on to your patch. To roll with those kinds of punches and endure in business takes something special.

It's no surprise to me that sport has been such a good training ground for people like Sir Jackie Stewart and David Lloyd. Lessons from sport can often be applied to business – identifying your opponent's weaknesses, practising until you get it right, preparing for every eventuality – but I hadn't expected to see just how often the factors that secure success in one arena are mirrored in the other. In fact, the biggest difference between sporting and business success is talent.

My talent was for rowing. Federer's is for tennis. Sir James Dyson's is for engineering. Sir Martin Sorrell's is for deal-making. Sir Jackie Stewart's is for bringing people together. All the other factors in our success – hard work, vision, belief, drive – are shared, and I'd be willing to bet that they are necessary for success no matter what your walk of life.

Of all the different elements of enduring success that I have written about in this book, I think there are three that are the most significant. Talent is the first. Without some modicum of ability for your chosen field, no amount of training or dedication will be enough. The second is hard work. Overnight success might happen by fluke, but long-term results are unavoidably linked to hard work – and lots of it. The third is enjoying what you do. If you don't get pleasure from your day-to-day job, you are never going to have the motivation to over-come obstacles or the enthusiasm to spot opportunities.

The best way of attaining enduring success is to find a role for yourself where your skills fit the opportunity.

If you can find the work you were born to do, then hard graft never seems like too much of a slog and the fun comes naturally. Those of us who can find a way of turning our talent into a career are both pretty smart, and incredibly lucky.

INDEX

Note: Page numbers in **bold** denote major sections.